PRIMARY MATHEMATICS 3A

Third Edition

Primary Mathematics Project Team

Project Director
Dr Kho Tek Hong

Team Members
Chee Kum Hoong, Hector
Chip Wai Lung
Liang Hin Hoon
Lim Eng Tann
Lim Hui Cheng, Rosalind
Ng Hwee Wan
Ng Siew Lee

Curriculum Specialists
Cheong Ngan Peng, Christina
Ho Juan Beng
Sin Kwai Meng

Curriculum Planning & Development Division
Ministry of Education, Singapore

FEDERAL PUBLICATIONS
An imprint of Times Media

P9-CAO-908

© 1982, 1992 Curriculum Development Institute of Singapore
© 1997, 1999 Curriculum Planning & Development Division
   Ministry of Education, Singapore

Published by
Times Media Private Limited
A member of the Times Publishing Group
Times Centre
1 New Industrial Road
Singapore 536196
E-mail: fps@tpl.com.sg
Online Book Store: http://www.timesone.com.sg/fpl

First published   1982
Second Edition 1992
Third Edition   1999
Reprinted   1999, 2000, 2001 (twice)

All rights reserved. No part of this publication may be
reproduced, stored in a retrieval system, or transmitted,
in any form or by any means, electronic, mechanical,
photocopying, recording or otherwise, without the prior
permission of the publishers.

ISBN 981 01 8049 7

Printed by Times Offset (M) Sdn. Bhd

Illustrator
Paul Yong

ACKNOWLEDGEMENTS

The project team would like to record their thanks to the following:

- members of the Primary Mathematics Team who developed the first edition and second edition of the package

- members of the Steering Committee for the second edition of the package

- teachers who tested the materials in the package and provided useful insights and suggestions

- Educational Technology Division, for the design and production of the audio-visual components of the package

- all those who have helped in one way or another in the development and production of the package

PREFACE

The Primary Mathematics Package comprises textbooks, workbooks, teacher's guides and audio-visual materials.

The main feature of the package is the use of the **Concrete** ➡ **Pictorial** ➡ **Abstract** approach. The pupils are provided with the necessary learning experiences beginning with the concrete and pictorial stages, followed by the abstract stage to enable them to learn mathematics meaningfully. Like the previous editions of the package, this edition encourages active thinking processes, communication of mathematical ideas and problem solving.

This textbook is accompanied by two workbooks and a teacher's guide. It comprises 5 units. Each unit is divided into parts: **1**, **2**, . . . Each part starts with a meaningful situation for communication and is followed by specific learning tasks numbered 1, 2, . . . The sign Workbook Exercise is used to link the textbook to the workbook exercises.

Practice exercises are designed to provide the pupils with further practice after they have done the relevant workbook exercises. Review exercises and revision exercises are provided for cumulative reviews of concepts and skills. All the practice exercises, review exercises and revision exercises are optional exercises.

The colour patch ■ is used to invite active participation from the pupils and to facilitate oral discussion. The pupils are advised not to write on the colour patches.

CONTENTS

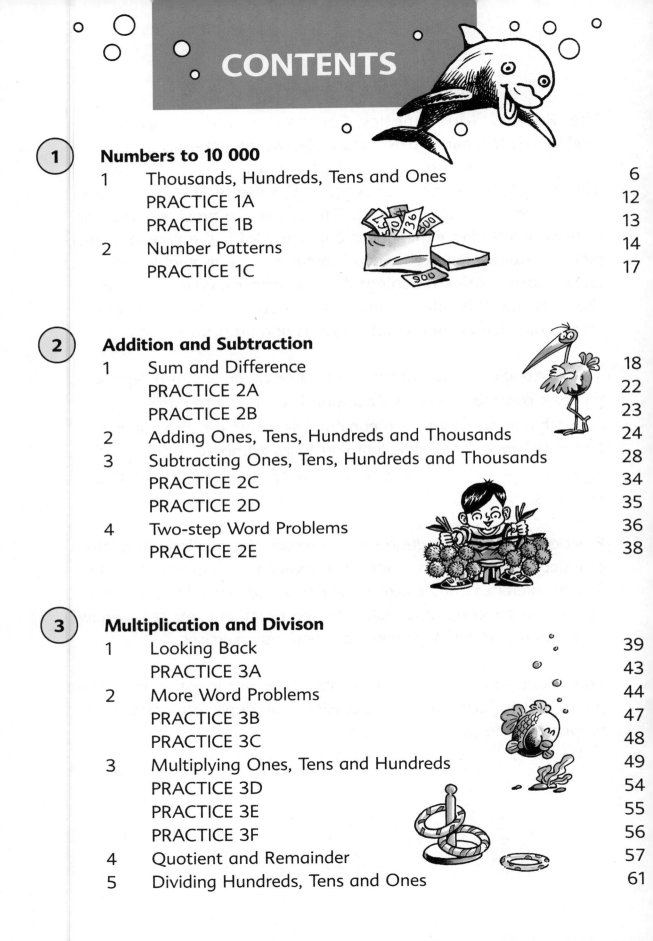

Numbers to 10 000

1 Thousands, Hundreds, Tens and Ones

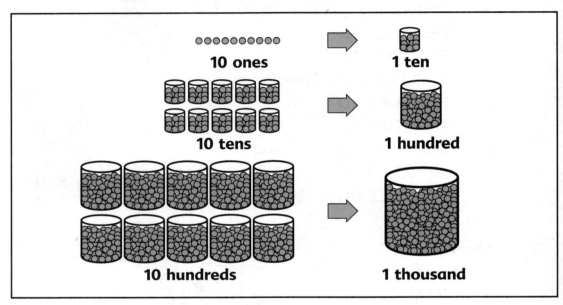

10 ones	1 ten
10 tens	1 hundred
10 hundreds	1 thousand

(a) Sumin collected some marbles.

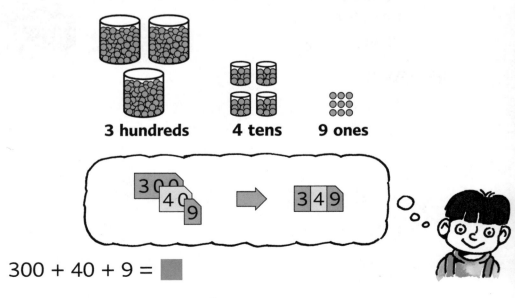

3 hundreds   4 tens   9 ones

300 + 40 + 9 = ▢

6

(b) His sister also collected some marbles.

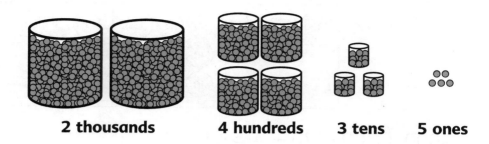

2 thousands   **4 hundreds**   **3 tens**   **5 ones**

2000 + 400 + 30 + 5 = ▇
How many marbles did she collect?

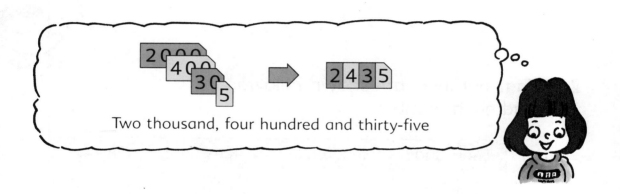

Two thousand, four hundred and thirty-five

(c) Read the numbers 5998 and 6012.

(d) Count from 5998 to 6012.

5998, 5999, 6000, ...6012.

(e) Count from 9987 to 10,000.

1. Count the thousands, hundreds, tens and ones in this chart.

Thousands	Hundreds	Tens	Ones
(1000) (1000) (1000)	(100) (100)	(10) (10) (10) (10) (10) (10) (10)	(1) (1) (1) (1)

3000 + 200 + 70 + 4 = ▮

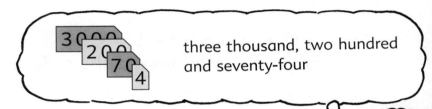

three thousand, two hundred and seventy-four

2. What numbers are shown below?
   Read each number.

(a)

Thousands	Hundreds	Tens	Ones
(1000) (1000)		(10) (10) (10) (10)	(1) (1) (1) (1) (1)

(b)

Thousands	Hundreds	Tens	Ones
(1000)	(100) (100) (100)		(1) (1) (1) (1) (1) (1) (1)

(c)

Thousands	Hundreds	Tens	Ones
(1000) (1000) (1000) (1000)	(100) (100)	(10) (10) (10) (10) (10)	

Workbook Exercise 1

3.

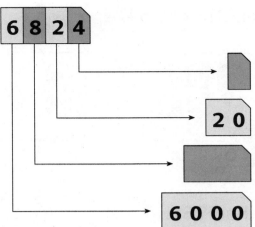

6824 is a 4-digit number.
The digit 2 stands for 20.
The digit 6 stands for 6000.
What does the digit 8 stand for?
What does the digit 4 stand for?

4. What does the digit **5** stand for in each of the following numbers?
    (a) 3**5**21   (b) **5**213   (c) 12**5**3

5.

Thousands	Hundreds	Tens	Ones
3	4	6	8

In 3468, the digit 8 is in the **ones place**.
Its **value** is 8.

The digit 6 is in the **tens place**.
Its value is 60.

The digit ▥ is in the **hundreds place**.
Its value is ▥.

The digit ▥ is in the **thousands place**.
Its value is ▥.

6. What is the value of each digit in 8137?

Workbook Exercise 2

7. Which is greater, 316 or 264?

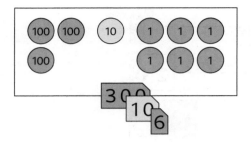 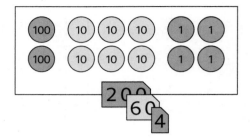

316 is greater than 264.

Which is smaller, 325 or 352?

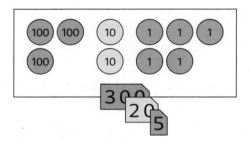 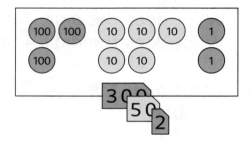

325 is smaller than 352.

(a) Which is greater, 4316 or 4264?
    Which is greater, 4316 or 5264?
(b) Which is smaller, 2325 or 2352?
    Which is smaller, 3325 or 2352?

8. Write the word **greater** or **smaller** in place of each ▨.
   (a) 7031 is ▨ than 7301.
   (b) 8004 is ▨ than 8040.
   (c) 3756 is ▨ than 3576.

9.   5073,   4982,   4973
   Which is the greatest number?
   Which is the smallest number?

10.

100 is the smallest 3-digit number.

999 is the greatest 3-digit number.

What is the smallest 4-digit number?
What is the greatest 4-digit number?

11. Arrange the numbers in order:

3412,   3142,   4123,   2431

Begin with the greatest.

12. Arrange the numbers in order:

1892,   9003,   913,   1703

Begin with the smallest.

13. Use all the digits 0, 4 and 5 to make different 3-digit numbers. Which is the greatest number? Which is the smallest number?

Do not begin a number with 0.

14. (a) What is the greatest 4-digit number that you can make using all the digits 0, 7, 2 and 8?
  (b) What is the smallest 4-digit number that you can make using all the digits 3, 7, 4 and 9?

Workbook Exercise 3

PRACTICE 1A

1. Write the numbers.
   (a) Two thousand, one hundred and sixty-three
   (b) Eight thousand and eight
   (c) Three thousand and six hundred
   (d) One thousand, three hundred and seventy-six
   (e) Four thousand and five

2. Write the numbers in words.
   (a) 1347   (b) 5900   (c) 7058

3. Write the numbers in thousands, hundreds, tens and ones.
   (a) 6352   (b) 4091   (c) 7004

4. What number is shown in each of the following?

   (a) (1000) (100) (100) (1) (1) (1) (1) (1)

   (b) (1000) (1000) (1000) (10) (10)

   (c) (1000) (1000) (10) (10) (10) (1) (1)

5. Find the missing numbers.
   (a) $1000 + 700 + 30 + 6 =$ ▨
   (b) $7000 + 500 + 4 =$ ▨
   (c) $3000 +$ ▨ $= 3090$
   (d) $6000 +$ ▨ $+ 2 = 6802$
   (e) $4243 = 4000 + 200 + 40 +$ ▨
   (f) $4907 -$ ▨ $= 4007$

6. Write the underlined words in figures.
   (a) The height of Mount Fuji in Japan is <u>three thousand, seven hundred and seventy-six</u> metres.
   (b) Mr Wang bought a computer for <u>two thousand and sixty</u> dollars.

PRACTICE 1B

1. Write the word **greater** or **smaller** in place of each ▇.
   (a) 7865 is ▇ than 8567
   (b) 4104 is ▇ than 4049
   (c) 3590 is ▇ than 3509
   (d) 9989 is ▇ than 9998
   (e) 7080 is ▇ than 7100
   (f) 2000 is ▇ than 10 000

2. Which is the greatest number in each of the following?
   (a) 7171,   7711,   7117
   (b) 8218,   8812,   8128

3. Which is the smallest number in each of the following?
   (a) 9909,   9099,   9990
   (b) 8544,   8454,   8445

4. Arrange these numbers in order, beginning with the greatest.

208   989   1260   1098

5. Arrange these numbers in order, beginning with the smallest.

3500   3050   5003   350   3005

2 Number Patterns

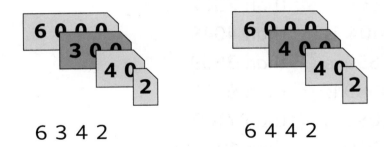

6 3 4 2   6 4 4 2

Which is more? How many more?

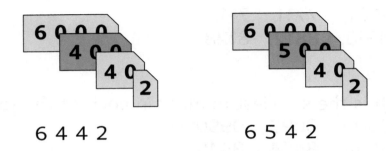

6 4 4 2   6 5 4 2

Which is more? How many more?

What number is 100 more than 6442?

What number is 100 more than 6542?

Complete the number pattern.

(a) 6342, 6442, 6542, ▮, ▮
(b) 6342, 7342, 8342, ▮, ▮
(c) 6342, 6343, 6344, ▮, ▮
(d) 6342, 6352, 6362, ▮, ▮

1. (a) What number is 100 more than 3624?

Thousands	Hundreds	Tens	Ones
1000 1000 1000	100 100 100 100 100 100	10 10	1 1 1 1

$$3624 \xrightarrow{\ +\ 100\ } \blacksquare$$

Add 1 hundred to 3624.

(b) What number is 1 more than 3624?
(c) What number is 10 more than 3624?
(d) What number is 1000 more than 3624?

2. (a) What number is 1000 less than 5732?

Thousands	Hundreds	Tens	Ones
1000 1000 1000 1000	100 100 100 100 100 100 100	10 10 10	1 1

$$5732 \xrightarrow{\ -\ 1000\ } \blacksquare$$

Subtract 1 thousand from 5732.

(b) What number is 1 less than 5732?
(c) What number is 10 less than 5732?
(d) What number is 100 less than 5732?

3. (a) Count in steps of 10 from 1678 to 1728.

   1678, 1688, 1698, ..., 1728.

   (b) Count in steps of 100 from 1678 to 2178.

   1678, 1778, 1878, ..., 2178.

   (c) Count in steps of 1000 from 1678 to 8678.

   1678, 2678, 3678, ..., 8678.

4. Complete the following number patterns.

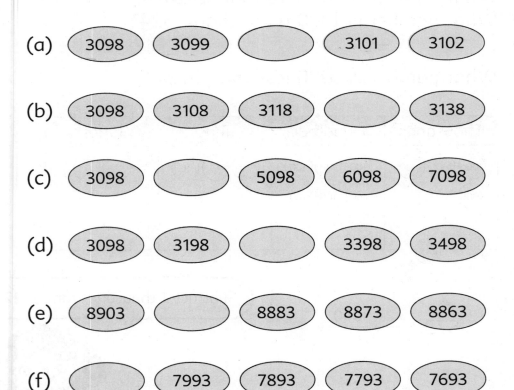

(a) 3098 3099 ( ) 3101 3102

(b) 3098 3108 3118 ( ) 3138

(c) 3098 ( ) 5098 6098 7098

(d) 3098 3198 ( ) 3398 3498

(e) 8903 ( ) 8883 8873 8863

(f) ( ) 7993 7893 7793 7693

Workbook Exercise 4

PRACTICE 1C

1. What is the value of the digit **8** in each of the following?
   (a) 7**8**92   (b) 346**8**   (c) **8**005   (d) 70**8**1

2. What does each digit in 5629 stand for?

3. (a) In 6243, the digit ▢ is in the **tens place**.
       Its value is ▢.
   (b) In 5029, the digit ▢ is in the **hundreds place**.
       Its value is ▢.

4. Write the next three numbers for each of the following number patterns.
   (a) 2007, 2008, 2009, ▢, ▢, ▢
   (b) 5612, 5622, 5632, ▢, ▢, ▢
   (c) 1800, 1900, 2000, ▢, ▢, ▢
   (d) 4056, 5056, 6056, ▢, ▢, ▢

5. Complete the following number patterns.
   (a) 997, 998, 999, ▢
   (b) 2008, ▢, 2010, 2011
   (c) 5760, 5770, ▢, 5790
   (d) 4800, 4900, ▢, 5100
   (e) 3040, ▢, 5040, 6040

6. Complete the following number patterns.
   (a) ▢, 5400, 5401, 5402
   (b) 3420, ▢, 3620, 3720
   (c) 4350, 3350, ▢, 1350
   (d) 8160, 7160, 6160, ▢
   (e) 5722, 5712, 5702, ▢

2

Addition and Subtraction

1 Sum and Difference

(a) What is the sum of 4 and 7?

$$4 + 7 = \blacksquare$$

To find the sum, we add the two numbers.

The sum of 4 and 7 is $\blacksquare$.

(b) What is the difference between 4 and 7?

$$7 - 4 = \blacksquare$$

To find the difference, we subtract the smaller number from the bigger number.

The difference between 4 and 7 is $\blacksquare$.

1.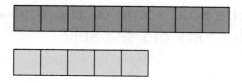

   (a) $8 + 5 = $ ▨

   The sum of 8 and 5 is ▨.

   (b) $8 - 5 = $ ▨

   The difference between 8 and 5 is ▨.

2.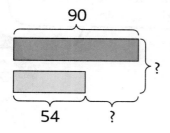

   (a) The sum of 90 and 54 is ▨.

   (b) The difference between 90 and 54 is ▨.

3. (a) The sum of 12 and 9 is ▨.

   (b) The sum of two numbers is 21.
   If one number is 9, the other number is ▨.

   (c) The difference between 21 and 9 is ▨.

   (d) The difference between 21 and 12 is ▨.

Workbook Exercise 5

4. Mary made 686 biscuits. She sold some of them. If 298 were left over, how many biscuits did she sell?

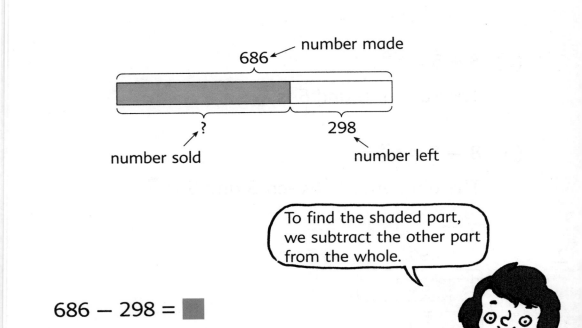

To find the shaded part, we subtract the other part from the whole.

$686 - 298 = $ ▨

She sold ▨ biscuits.

5. A man sold 230 balloons at a funfair in the morning.
He sold another 86 balloons in the evening.
How many balloons did he sell in all?

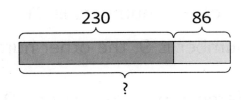

$230 + 86 = $ ▨

He sold ▨ balloons in all.

6.   134 girls and 119 boys took part in an art competition.
     How many more girls than boys were there?

     134 − 119 = ■

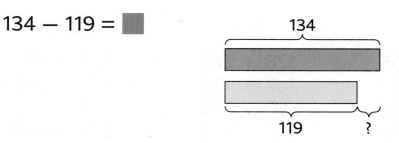

     There were ■ more girls than boys.

7.   Meilin saved $184.
     She saved $63 more than Betty.
     How much did Betty save?

     184 − 63 = ■

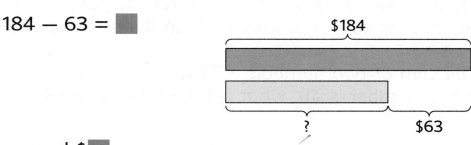

     Betty saved $■.

     Workbook Exercise 6

8.   John read 32 pages in the morning.
     He read 14 pages less in the afternoon.
     (a) How many pages did he read in the afternoon?
     (b) How many pages did he read altogether?

     (a) 32 − 14 = 18
          He read 18 pages in the afternoon.

     (b) 32 + 18 = 50
          He read 50 pages altogether.

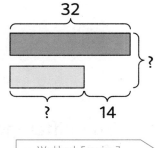

     Workbook Exercise 7

PRACTICE 2A

Find the value of each of the following:

	(a)	(b)	(c)
1.	509 + 365	128 + 280	384 + 418
2.	746 + 254	262 + 138	432 + 368
3.	715 − 235	800 − 236	308 − 153
4.	514 − 266	600 − 162	504 − 354

5. Leela has 254 rubber bands.
    Her friend gives her 58 more.
    How many rubber bands has she now?

6. A man bought 650 curry puffs for a party.
    There were 39 curry puffs left after the party.
    How many curry puffs were eaten during the party?

7. The sum of two numbers is 175.
    If one number is 49, what is the other number?

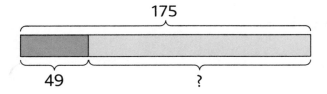

8. The difference between two numbers is 68.
    If the smaller number is 153, what is the bigger number?

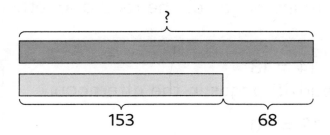

9. The difference between two numbers is 48.
    If the bigger number is 126, what is the smaller number?

PRACTICE 2B

Find the value of each of the following:

	(a)	(b)	(c)
1.	730 + 313	305 + 179	265 + 161
2.	724 + 184	310 + 184	668 + 475
3.	746 − 316	310 − 187	600 − 382
4.	470 − 371	627 − 298	374 − 361

5. Mr Wang paid $850 for a television set.
He still had $450 left.
How much money had he at first?

6. 429 concert tickets were sold on Sunday.
64 more concert tickets were sold on Sunday than on Saturday.
How many tickets were sold on Saturday?

7. This table shows the number of biscuits made by three machines in one hour.

Machine A	468
Machine B	652
Machine C	945

   (a) What is the total number of biscuits made by Machine A and Machine B?
   (b) What is the total number of biscuits made by the three machines?

8. Ravi had 35 tickets to sell.
He sold 15 tickets yesterday and 9 tickets today.
   (a) How many tickets did he sell on the two days?
   (b) How many tickets were **not** sold?

9. David collected 830 saga seeds.
Peter collected 177 fewer saga seeds than David.
   (a) How many saga seeds did Peter collect?
   (b) How many saga seeds did they collect altogether?

Adding Ones, Tens, Hundreds and Thousands

Find the sum of 2803 and 1443.

$$2803$$
$$+\ 1443$$

Thousands	Hundreds	Tens	Ones
1000 1000 1000	100 100 100 / 100 100 100 / 100 100 / 100 100 100 / 100	10 10 10 / 10	1 1 1 / 1 1 1

1000 1000 / 1000 1000	100 100	10 10 10 / 10	1 1 1 / 1 1 1

As there are more than 10 hundreds, we change 10 hundreds for 1 thousand.

2803 + 1443 = **6**	2803 + 1443 = **4**6	$\overset{1}{2}$803 + 1443 = **2**46	$\overset{1}{2}$803 + 1443 = **4**246
Add the ones.	**Add the tens.**	**Add the hundreds.**	**Add the thousands.**

1. Find the value of
   (a) 4263 + 5   (b) 4263 + 20
   (c) 4263 + 400   (d) 4263 + 3000
   (e) 4263 + 425   (f) 4263 + 3425

2. 2048 + 2 =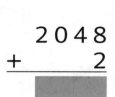

```
  2 0 4 8
+       2
```

Thousands	Hundreds	Tens	Ones
1000 1000		10 10 10	1 1 1
		10 10	1 1 1
			1 1
			1 1

3. 5840 + 60 =

```
  5 8 4 0
+     6 0
```

Thousands	Hundreds	Tens	Ones
1000 1000 1000	100 100 100	10 10 10	
1000 1000	100 100	10	
	100 100		
	100 100	10 10 10	
		10 10 10	

4. 3700 + 300 =

```
  3 7 0 0
+   3 0 0
```

Thousands	Hundreds	Tens	Ones
1000 1000	100 100 100		
1000	100 100 100		
1000	100		
	100 100 100		

5. Find the value of
(a) 1028 + 234
(b) 2409 + 1245
(c) 4190 + 649
(d) 3260 + 4282
(e) 6204 + 993
(f) 5402 + 2960

Workbook Exercise 8

6. Find the sum of 1266 and 2355.

$$\begin{array}{r} 1\,2\,6\,6 \\ +\ 2\,3\,5\,5 \\ \hline \end{array}$$

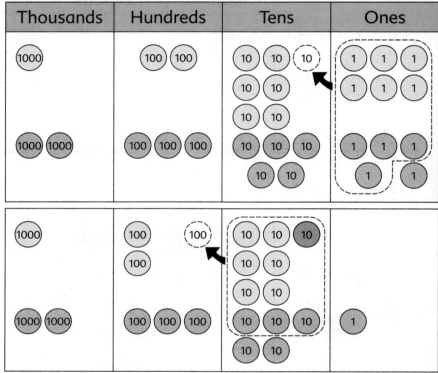

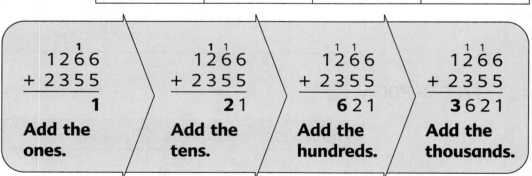

$\begin{array}{r}\overset{1}{1}2\,6\,6 \\ +\ 2\,3\,5\,5 \\ \hline 1\end{array}$	$\begin{array}{r}\overset{1}{1}\overset{1}{2}\,6\,6 \\ +\ 2\,3\,5\,5 \\ \hline 2\,1\end{array}$	$\begin{array}{r}\overset{1}{1}\overset{1}{2}\,6\,6 \\ +\ 2\,3\,5\,5 \\ \hline 6\,2\,1\end{array}$	$\begin{array}{r}\overset{1}{1}\overset{1}{2}\,6\,6 \\ +\ 2\,3\,5\,5 \\ \hline 3\,6\,2\,1\end{array}$
Add the ones.	**Add the tens.**	**Add the hundreds.**	**Add the thousands.**

7. Find the value of
(a) 1326 + 194
(b) 3762 + 5158
(c) 5471 + 787
(d) 6942 + 1095
(e) 7246 + 845
(f) 4653 + 2729

8. Find the sum of 3589 and 2443.

```
  3 5 8 9
+ 2 4 4 3
```

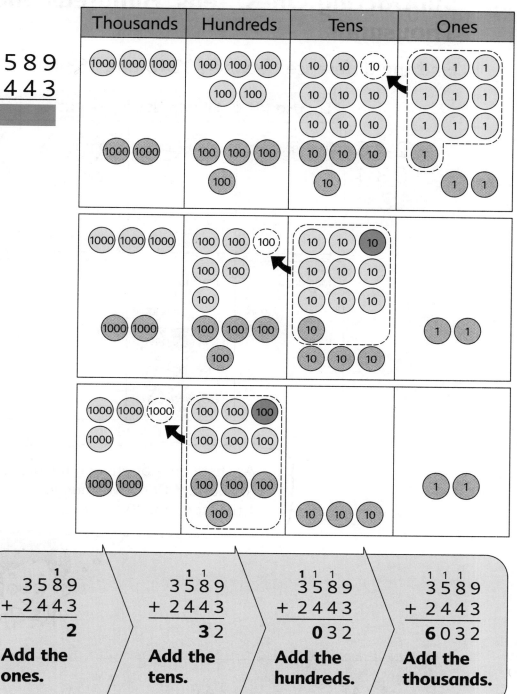

	3589		3589		3589		3589
	+ 2443		+ 2443		+ 2443		+ 2443
	2		32		032		6032
	Add the ones.		**Add the tens.**		**Add the hundreds.**		**Add the thousands.**

9. Find the value of
   (a) 4697 + 1316   (b) 3587 + 3813
   (c) 2908 + 5892   (d) 2824 + 2576

Workbook Exercise 9

27

Subtracting Ones, Tens, Hundreds and Thousands

Find the difference between 3246 and 1634.

Thousands	Hundreds	Tens	Ones
(1000) (1000) (1000)	(100) (100)	~~10~~ ~~10~~ ~~10~~	~~1~~ ~~1~~ ~~1~~
		10	~~1~~ 1 1

$$
\begin{array}{r}
3\,2\,4\,6 \\
-\,1\,6\,3\,4 \\
\hline
\end{array}
$$

Thousands	Hundreds	Tens	Ones
~~(1000)~~ (1000)	(100) (100)	10	1 1
(1000) →	100 / 100 100 100 / 100 100 100 / 100 100 100		

As there are not enough hundreds to subtract from, we change 1 thousand for 10 hundreds.

Subtract the ones.	Subtract the tens.	Subtract the hundreds.	Subtract the thousands.
$\begin{array}{r} 3246 \\ -1634 \\ \hline 2 \end{array}$	$\begin{array}{r} 3246 \\ -1634 \\ \hline 12 \end{array}$	$\begin{array}{r} {}^{2}\ {}^{12} \\ 3\cancel{2}46 \\ -1634 \\ \hline 612 \end{array}$	$\begin{array}{r} {}^{2}\ {}^{12} \\ 3\cancel{2}46 \\ -1634 \\ \hline 1612 \end{array}$

1. Find the value of
   (a) 6847 − 3
   (b) 6847 − 20
   (c) 6847 − 500
   (d) 6847 − 4000
   (e) 6847 − 523
   (f) 6847 − 4523

2. 5340 − 6 = ◼

$$\begin{array}{r} 5\,3\,4\,0 \\ -\qquad 6 \\ \hline \end{array}$$

Thousands	Hundreds	Tens	Ones
1000 1000 1000 1000 1000	100 100 100	10 10 10 10	1 1 1 1 1 1 1 1 1 1

3. 4500 − 80 = ◼

$$\begin{array}{r} 4\,5\,0\,0 \\ -\qquad 8\,0 \\ \hline \end{array}$$

Thousands	Hundreds	Tens	Ones
1000 1000 1000 1000	100 100 100 100 100	10 10 10 10 10 10 10 10 10 10	

4. 7000 − 300 = ◼

$$\begin{array}{r} 7\,0\,0\,0 \\ -\quad 3\,0\,0 \\ \hline \end{array}$$

Thousands	Hundreds	Tens	Ones
1000 1000 1000 1000 1000 1000 1000	100 100 100 100 100 100 100 100 100 100		

29

5. Find the value of
    (a) 4821 − 514   (b) 5645 − 1317
    (c) 6743 − 461   (d) 8769 − 3292
    (e) 9674 − 853   (f) 7356 − 4731

Workbook Exercise 10

6. Find the difference between 2435 and 1268.

$$\begin{array}{r} 2435 \\ -\ 1268 \\ \hline \end{array}$$

Thousands	Hundreds	Tens	Ones
1000 1000	100 100 100 100	10 10 10	1 1 1 1 1 1 1
1000 1000	100 100 100 100	10 10 10 10 10 10 10 10 10	1 1 1 1 1 1 1

$$\begin{array}{r} {}^{2\ 15} \\ 24\cancel{3}\cancel{5} \\ -\ 1268 \\ \hline 7 \end{array}$$
Subtract the ones.

$$\begin{array}{r} {}^{3\ 12\ 15} \\ 2\cancel{4}\cancel{3}\cancel{5} \\ -\ 1268 \\ \hline 67 \end{array}$$
Subtract the tens.

$$\begin{array}{r} {}^{3\ 12\ 15} \\ 2\cancel{4}\cancel{3}\cancel{5} \\ -\ 1268 \\ \hline 167 \end{array}$$
Subtract the hundreds.

$$\begin{array}{r} {}^{3\ 12\ 15} \\ 2\cancel{4}\cancel{3}\cancel{5} \\ -\ 1268 \\ \hline 1167 \end{array}$$
Subtract the thousands.

7. Find the value of
    (a) 7613 − 185   (b) 8450 − 4262
    (c) 4581 − 790   (d) 9608 − 6894
    (e) 6094 − 428   (f) 3640 − 1807

30

8. Find the difference between 5243 and 2787.

$$5243$$
$$-2787$$

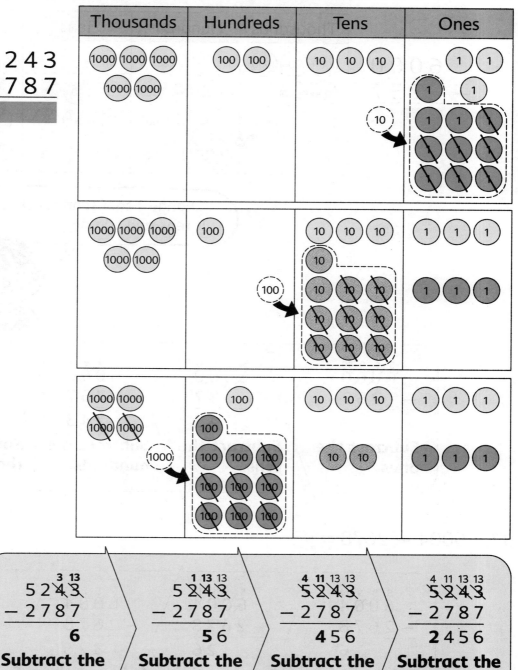

9. Find the value of
   (a) 7165 − 5268
   (b) 6875 − 3996
   (c) 8353 − 3572
   (d) 9564 − 8467

Workbook Exercise 11

10. Find the difference between 6000 and 257.

$$\begin{array}{r} 6\,0\,0\,0 \\ -\ \ 2\,5\,7 \\ \hline \end{array}$$

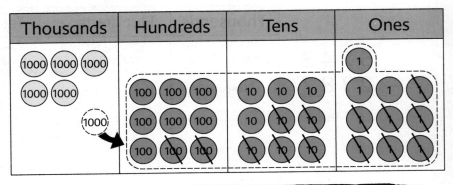

Change 1 thousand for 9 hundreds,
9 tens and 10 ones.

| $\overset{5\ 9\ 9\ 10}{\cancel{6\,0\,0\,0}}$ $-\ \ 2\,5\,7$ **3** **Subtract the ones.** | $\overset{5\ 9\ 9\ 10}{\cancel{6\,0\,0\,0}}$ $-\ \ 2\,5\,7$ **4** 3 **Subtract the tens.** | $\overset{5\ 9\ 9\ 10}{\cancel{6\,0\,0\,0}}$ $-\ \ 2\,5\,7$ **7** 4 3 **Subtract the hundreds.** | $\overset{5\ 9\ 9\ 10}{\cancel{6\,0\,0\,0}}$ $-\ \ 2\,5\,7$ **5** 7 4 3 **Subtract the thousands.** |

11. 6004 − 2678 = ▨

| $\overset{5\ 9\ 9\ 14}{\cancel{6\,0\,0\,4}}$ $-\,2\,6\,7\,8$ **6** **Subtract the ones.** | $\overset{5\ 9\ 9\ 14}{\cancel{6\,0\,0\,4}}$ $-\,2\,6\,7\,8$ **2** 6 **Subtract the tens.** | $\overset{5\ 9\ 9\ 14}{\cancel{6\,0\,0\,4}}$ $-\,2\,6\,7\,8$ **3** 2 6 **Subtract the hundreds.** | $\overset{5\ 9\ 9\ 14}{\cancel{6\,0\,0\,4}}$ $-\,2\,6\,7\,8$ **3** 3 2 6 **Subtract the thousands.** |

12. Find the value of
    (a) 4000 − 392
    (b) 7002 − 4847
    (c) 3020 − 2430
    (d) 5000 − 2074

13. $5200 - 948 = \blacksquare$

$$\begin{array}{r} 5200 \\ -\ 948 \\ \hline \blacksquare \end{array}$$

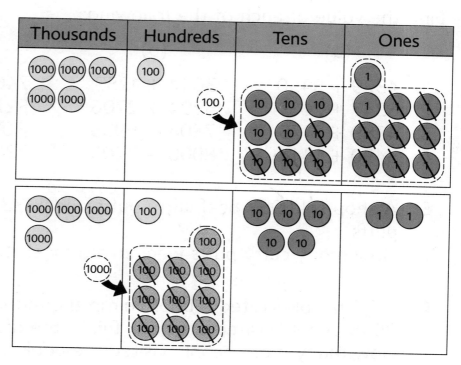

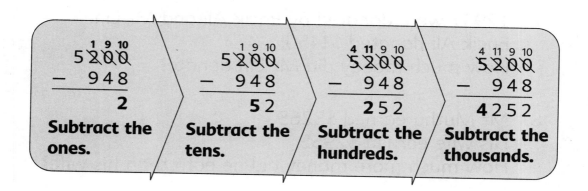

Subtract the ones. Subtract the tens. Subtract the hundreds. Subtract the thousands.

14. Find the value of
   (a) $8007 - 3429$
   (b) $6900 - 745$
   (c) $9403 - 4275$
   (d) $5302 - 4618$
   (e) $7063 - 5476$
   (f) $10\ 000 - 5721$

Workbook Exercise 12

PRACTICE 2C

Find the value of each of the following:

	(a)	(b)	(c)
1.	4329 + 5450	3642 + 1253	7465 − 3214
2.	6347 + 2613	5294 + 2706	5277 − 1863
3.	4389 + 3175	7804 − 6935	8016 − 5452
4.	3490 + 1844	8000 − 3405	3378 − 2499

5. A shop sold 957 beef curry puffs and 1238 chicken curry puffs.
   How many curry puffs were sold altogether?

6. 1730 people visited a book fair in the morning.
   2545 people visited the book fair in the afternoon.
   How many more people visited the book fair in the afternoon than in the morning?

7. $2937 were donated by Encik Ali and Mr Lin.
   Encik Ali donated $1450.
   How much money did Mr Lin donate?

8. Mr Muthu earned $3265.
   His wife earned $2955.
   How much more money did he earn than his wife?

9. 1147 people went to Sentosa by cable car.
   3996 more people went to Sentosa by ferry than by cable car.
   How many people went to Sentosa by ferry?

10. Alice saved $2900.
    She saved $1567 less than her brother.
    How much did her brother save?

PRACTICE 2D

Find the value of each of the following:

	(a)	(b)	(c)
1.	6203 + 977	2645 + 3875	8300 − 4251
2.	5472 + 4415	4975 + 1928	9613 − 5357
3.	2446 + 6596	7042 − 5170	3142 − 1455
4.	3421 + 4282	9000 − 6571	7173 − 3654

5. There were 2055 people at a concert.
   1637 of them were adults.
   How many children were there?

6. There are 1206 pupils in a school.
   47 of them were absent yesterday.
   How many pupils were present?

7. Out of 2316 tickets sold, 1548 tickets were for a football match.
   The rest were for a badminton match.
   How many tickets for the badminton match were sold?

8. The table shows the prices of two pianos.
   How much cheaper is Piano B than Piano A?

Piano A	$2005
Piano B	$1542

9. Encik Rahmat had $5000.
   He spent $2572 on a computer and $955 on a television set.
   (a) How much money did he spend?
   (b) How much money had he left?

10. In a school, there are 1225 pupils in the morning session and 904 pupils in the afternoon session.
    (a) How many fewer pupils are in the afternoon session than in the morning session?
    (b) How many pupils are there altogether?

4 Two-step Word Problems

James picked 17 rambutans and Liming picked 12.
They ate 20 of the rambutans.
How many rambutans were left?

> Find the total number of rambutans they picked altogether first.

$$17 + 12 = 29$$

They picked 29 rambutans altogether.

$$29 - 20 = \blacksquare$$

$\blacksquare$ rambutans were left.

1. 125 children took part in a mathematics competition.
   54 of them were girls.
   How many more boys than girls were there?

   $125 - 54 = 71$

   Find the total number of boys first.

   There were 71 boys.

   $71 - 54 = $ ▧

   There were ▧ more boys than girls.

2. Ali collected 137 stamps.
   He collected 27 stamps less than his sister.
   How many stamps did they collect altogether?

   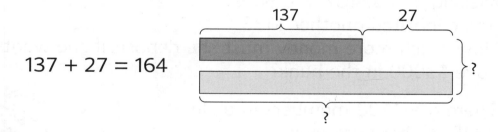

   $137 + 27 = 164$

   Ali's sister collected 164 stamps.

   $137 + 164 = $ ▧

   They collected ▧ stamps altogether.

Workbook Exercise 13

PRACTICE 2E

1. A farmer collected 1930 chicken eggs.
   He collected 859 fewer duck eggs than chicken eggs.
   How many eggs did he collect altogether?

2. 4100 children took part in an art competition.
   2680 of them were boys.
   How many more boys than girls were there?

3. Encik Ali made 1050 sticks of chicken
   satay and 950 sticks of mutton satay.
   He sold 1765 sticks of satay altogether.
   How many sticks of satay had he left?

4. Mr Li earned $3915.
   He spent $1268 on food and $1380 on rent and transport.
   How much did he have left?

5. A refrigerator costs $1739.
   An oven is $850 cheaper than the refrigerator.
   Mrs Chen buys both the refrigerator and the oven.
   How much does she pay?

6. Meiling had $2467 in a bank.
   She deposited another $133.
   How much more money must she deposit if she wants to
   have $3000 in the bank?

7. There are 4608 members in a club.
   2745 of them are men.
   855 are women.
   The rest are children.
   How many children are there?

8. Miss Li saved $1035.
   Miss Wang saved $278 more than Miss Li.
   Miss Wu saved $105 less than Miss Wang.
   How much did Miss Wu save?

Multiplication and Division

1 Looking Back

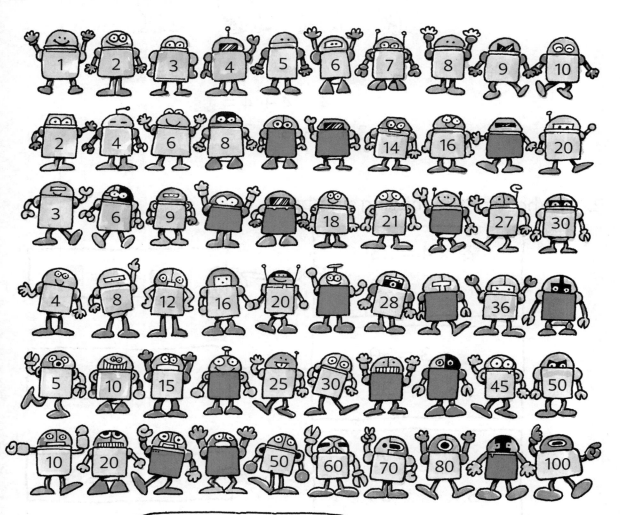

2 multiplied by 4 is 8.
What is 2 multiplied by 5?

1. Complete the number sentences.

$4 \times 3 =$ ▪ $3 \times 4 =$ ▪

$4 + 4 + 4 =$ ▪

$3 + 3 + 3 + 3 =$ ▪

Workbook Exercises 14 & 15

2. What are the missing numbers?

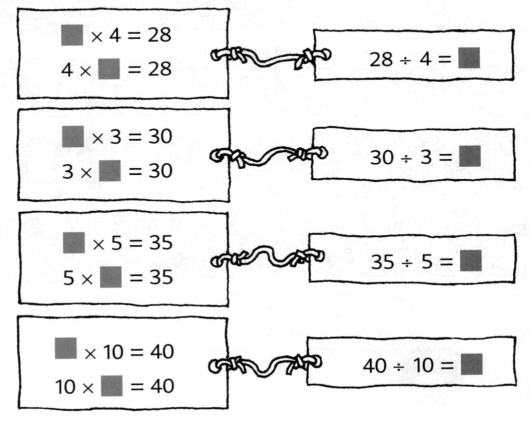

▪ $\times 4 = 28$

$4 \times$ ▪ $= 28$

$28 \div 4 =$ ▪

▪ $\times 3 = 30$

$3 \times$ ▪ $= 30$

$30 \div 3 =$ ▪

▪ $\times 5 = 35$

$5 \times$ ▪ $= 35$

$35 \div 5 =$ ▪

▪ $\times 10 = 40$

$10 \times$ ▪ $= 40$

$40 \div 10 =$ ▪

3. How many stars are there on each pair of cards?

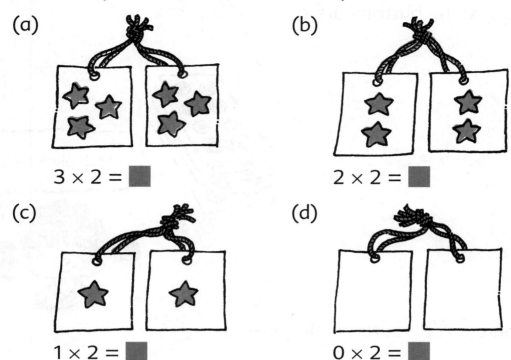

(a)

$3 \times 2 = \blacksquare$

(b)

$2 \times 2 = \blacksquare$

(c)

$1 \times 2 = \blacksquare$

(d)

$0 \times 2 = \blacksquare$

4. A player threw 3 rings over the post.
For each ring that was thrown in, the player scored 2 points.
How many points were scored in each of the following?

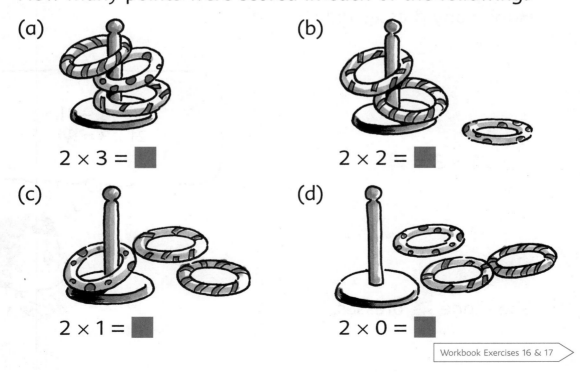

(a)

$2 \times 3 = \blacksquare$

(b)

$2 \times 2 = \blacksquare$

(c)

$2 \times 1 = \blacksquare$

(d)

$2 \times 0 = \blacksquare$

Workbook Exercises 16 & 17

5. There are 8 buttons on each card.
   How many buttons are there on 5 cards?

$8 \times 5 = \blacksquare$

Multiply 8 by 5.

There are $\blacksquare$ buttons altogether.

6. A tailor used 21 m of cloth to make dresses.
   She used 3 m of cloth for each dress.
   How many dresses did she make?

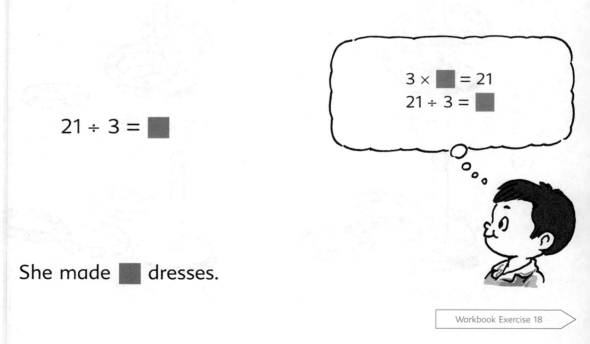

$3 \times \blacksquare = 21$

$21 \div 3 = \blacksquare$

$21 \div 3 = \blacksquare$

She made $\blacksquare$ dresses.

Workbook Exercise 18

PRACTICE 3A

Find the value of each of the following:

	(a)	(b)	(c)	(d)
1.	4×3	$16 \div 2$	0×4	$50 \div 10$
2.	5×6	$21 \div 3$	2×10	$0 \div 4$
3.	7×0	$36 \div 4$	4×9	$18 \div 2$

4. Mrs Fu bought 3 packets of strawberries.
   There were 8 strawberries in each packet.
   How many strawberries did she buy altogether?

5. Sumin arranged 24 toy soldiers in 4 rows.
   There were an equal number of toy soldiers in each row.
   How many toy soldiers were there in each row?

6. Devi saved $5 a week for 8 weeks.
   How much did she save altogether?

7. Cik Siti paid $18 for 3 kg of durians.
   What was the cost of 1 kg of durians?

8. Mrs Wu baked 6 cakes.
   She put 10 cherries on each cake.
   How many cherries did she use altogether?

9. David bought 4 pineapples at $3 each.
   How much did he pay altogether?

10. There were 27 desks to clean.
    3 boys shared the work equally.
    How many desks did each boy clean?

11. 3 children made 24 birthday cards altogether.
    Each child made the same number of cards.
    How many cards did each child make?

② More Word Problems

There are 9 white flowers.
There are 3 times as many red flowers as white flowers.
How many red flowers are there?

There are more red flowers than white flowers.

Multiply 9 by 3.

9

9 × 3

$9 \times 3 = 27$

There are ▊ red flowers.

1. Meihua has $16.
   She has twice as much money as Sulin.
   How much money does Sulin have?

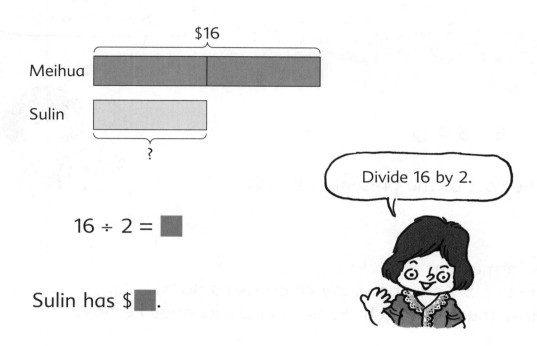

$16 \div 2 = \blacksquare$

Sulin has $\blacksquare$.

2. 4 children bought a present for $28.
   They shared the cost equally.
   How much did each child pay?

$28 \div 4 = \blacksquare$

Each child paid $\blacksquare$.

3. 5 children shared the cost of a present equally.
Each of them paid $6.
What was the cost of the present?

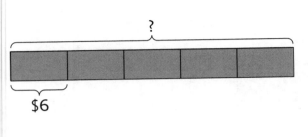

1 unit = $6
5 units = $6 × 5

$6

$6 × 5 = \blacksquare$

The cost of the present was $\blacksquare$.

Workbook Exercise 19

4. A farmer has 7 ducks.
He has 5 times as many chickens as ducks.
How many more chickens than ducks does he have?

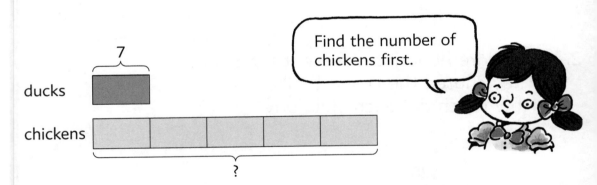

Find the number of chickens first.

ducks

7

chickens

?

$7 × 5 = 35$

He has 35 chickens.

$35 − 7 = \blacksquare$

He has $\blacksquare$ chickens more than ducks.

Workbook Exercise 20

PRACTICE 3B

Find the value of each of the following:

	(a)	(b)	(c)	(d)
1.	6 × 2	24 ÷ 3	2 × 7	32 ÷ 4
2.	7 × 3	14 ÷ 2	5 × 6	20 ÷ 5
3.	3 × 4	25 ÷ 5	4 × 8	28 ÷ 4
4.	7 × 5	16 ÷ 4	10 × 2	60 ÷ 10
5.	9 × 10	70 ÷ 10	3 × 9	36 ÷ 4

6. There are 6 rows of chairs.
   There are 30 chairs altogether.
   How many chairs are there in each row?

7. A toy car costs $6.
   A train set costs 5 times as much as the toy car.
   What is the cost of the train set?

8. Mrs Li bought 10 towels.
   Each towel cost $8.
   How much did she pay?

9. Hassan weighs 36 kg.
   He is 4 times as heavy as his brother.
   How heavy is his brother?

10. Mrs Wu bought 4 boxes of pencils.
    There were 5 blue pencils and 3 red pencils in each box.
    (a) How many pencils were there in each box?
    (b) How many pencils did Mrs Wu buy?

11. Miss Li marked 5 sets of 8 books in the morning.
    She marked 30 books in the afternoon.
    (a) How many books did she mark in the morning?
    (b) How many books did she mark altogether?

12. There are 9 red balloons.
    There are 3 times as many blue balloons as
    red balloons.
    How many balloons are there altogether?

PRACTICE 3C

Find the value of each of the following:

	(a)	(b)	(c)	(d)
1.	1×5	$14 \div 2$	6×3	$28 \div 4$
2.	9×2	$12 \div 4$	5×7	$40 \div 5$
3.	3×3	$0 \div 5$	3×8	$15 \div 3$
4.	8×4	$90 \div 10$	2×0	$70 \div 10$
5.	0×4	$21 \div 3$	4×6	$0 \div 2$

6. Ahmad earned $10 a day.
   He worked for 7 days.
   How much did he earn altogether?

7. Cik Fatimah bought 15 kg of rice.
   She bought 3 times as much rice as sugar.
   How many kilograms of sugar did she buy?

8. Devi practised on the piano for 2 hours each day.
   How many hours did she practise in 7 days?

9. Mrs Li poured 16 litres of syrup equally into 4 bottles.
   How many litres of syrup were there in each bottle?

10. Meihua has 6 postcards.
    Sumin has 3 times as many postcards as Meihua.
    How many more postcards does Sumin have than
    Meihua?

11. Minffa has 6 goldfish.
    He has 5 times as many guppies as
    goldfish.
    If he puts his guppies equally into 3 tanks,
    how many guppies are there in each tank?

12. Raju bought 18 pencils.
    He bought twice as many pencils as pens.
    How much did he pay for the pens if each pen cost $3?

48

3 Multiplying Ones, Tens and Hundreds

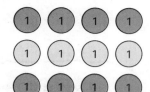

$4 \times 3 = 12$

Multiply 4 ones by 3:
4 ones × 3 = 12 ones

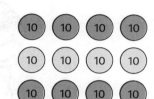

$40 \times 3 = \blacksquare$

Multiply 4 tens by 3:
4 tens × 3 = 12 tens

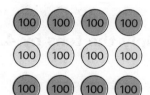

$400 \times 3 = \blacksquare$

Multiply 4 hundreds by 3:
4 hundreds × 3 = 12 hundreds

$\begin{array}{r} 4 \\ \times\ 3 \\ \hline 12 \end{array}$	$\begin{array}{r} 4\mathbf{0} \\ \times\ \ 3 \\ \hline 12\mathbf{0} \end{array}$	$\begin{array}{r} 4\mathbf{00} \\ \times\ \ \ 3 \\ \hline 12\mathbf{00} \end{array}$
12 ones	12 tens	12 hundreds

1. Find the value of
   (a) 9×5 (b) 90×5 (c) 900×5
   (d) 5×9 (e) 50×9 (f) 500×9

   Workbook Exercise 21

2. Multiply 12 by 4.

$12 \times 4 = 40 + 8$

$$\begin{array}{r} 12 \\ \times \quad 4 \\ \hline \end{array}$$

Tens	Ones
10 10 10 10	1 1 1 1 1 1 1 1
$10 \times 4 = 40$	$2 \times 4 = 8$

$$\begin{array}{r} 12 \\ \times \quad 4 \\ \hline 8 \end{array}$$
Multiply the ones by 4.

$$\begin{array}{r} 12 \\ \times \quad 4 \\ \hline 48 \end{array}$$
Multiply the tens by 4.

When we multiply 12 by 4, the **product** is 48.

48 is the **product of 12 and 4**.

3. Multiply 42 by 3.

 × 3

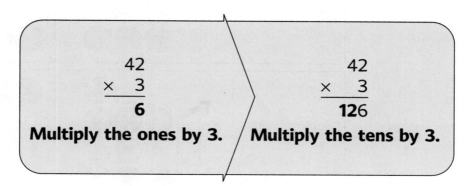

42
×   3

Hundreds	Tens	Ones

42
×   3
—
6

Multiply the ones by 3.

42
×   3
—
126

Multiply the tens by 3.

Workbook Exercise 22

4. Multiply 24 by 3.

 × 3

24
×   3

Hundreds	Tens	Ones

¹24
×   3
—
2

Multiply the ones by 3.

¹24
×   3
—
72

Multiply the tens by 3.

51

5. Multiply 34 by 3.

$$\begin{array}{r} 34 \\ \times\ 3 \\ \hline \end{array}$$

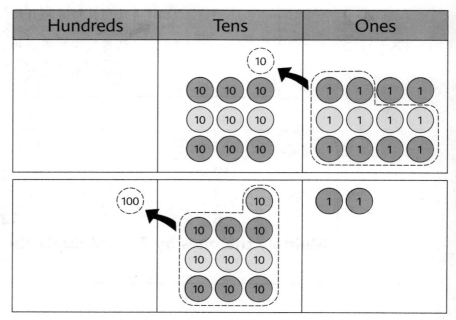

Hundreds	Tens	Ones

$$\begin{array}{r} {}^1 \\ 34 \\ \times\ 3 \\ \hline 2 \end{array}$$

Multiply the ones by 3.

$$\begin{array}{r} {}^1 \\ 34 \\ \times\ 3 \\ \hline \mathbf{10}2 \end{array}$$

Multiply the tens by 3.

6. Find the product for each of the following:
   (a) 81 × 2   (b) 16 × 3   (c) 3 × 37
   (d) 52 × 4   (e) 23 × 4   (f) 5 × 45
   (g) 63 × 3   (h) 24 × 5   (i) 4 × 38

Workbook Exercise 23

7. $3 \times 342 = \blacksquare$

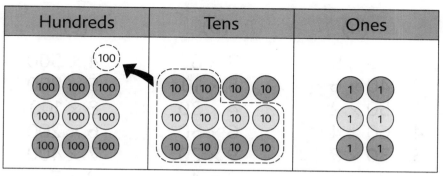

Hundreds	Tens	Ones

Multiply the ones by 3.
$$\begin{array}{r} 342 \\ \times \quad 3 \\ \hline 6 \end{array}$$
Multiply the ones by 3.

$$\begin{array}{r} {}^{1}342 \\ \times \quad 3 \\ \hline 26 \end{array}$$
Multiply the tens by 3.

$$\begin{array}{r} {}^{1}342 \\ \times \quad 3 \\ \hline 1026 \end{array}$$
Multiply the hundreds by 3.

8. Find the product of 245 and 3.

$$\begin{array}{r} {}^{1}245 \\ \times \quad 3 \\ \hline 5 \end{array}$$
Multiply the ones by 3.

$$\begin{array}{r} {}^{11}245 \\ \times \quad 3 \\ \hline 35 \end{array}$$
Multiply the tens by 3.

$$\begin{array}{r} {}^{11}245 \\ \times \quad 3 \\ \hline 735 \end{array}$$
Multiply the hundreds by 3.

9. Find the product for each of the following:
   (a) 214×2
   (b) 323×3
   (c) 4×231
   (d) 620×3
   (e) 451×2
   (f) 3×234
   (g) 289×3
   (h) 704×5
   (i) 5×436

Workbook Exercise 24

PRACTICE 3D

Find the value of each of the following:

	(a)	(b)	(c)	(d)
1.	20 × 9	3 × 80	4 × 500	200 × 5
2.	40 × 6	5 × 10	5 × 800	400 × 4
3.	50 × 2	4 × 30	8 × 100	300 × 5
4.	60 × 4	6 × 50	6 × 200	400 × 7
5.	30 × 8	9 × 20	7 × 400	500 × 4
6.	32 × 3	72 × 4	52 × 5	58 × 2
7.	2 × 49	4 × 43	3 × 75	5 × 43

8. A bookseller sold 30 books on the first day.
   On the second day, he sold 8 times as many books as on the first day.
   How many books did he sell on the second day?

9. Mingfa had 4 rolls of film.
   He took 24 pictures with each roll.
   How many pictures did he take altogether?

10. There are 5 rows of tiles.
    There are 56 tiles in each row.
    How many tiles are there altogether?

11. Meihua collected 76 stickers.
    Sulin collected 3 times as many stickers as Meihua.
    How many stickers did Sulin collect?

12. Devi bought 4 dolls at $38 each.
    How much did she pay altogether?

PRACTICE 3E

Find the value of each of the following:

	(a)	(b)	(c)	(d)
1.	300 × 4	3 × 312	419 × 5	4 × 550
2.	901 × 2	3 × 508	625 × 4	5 × 392
3.	614 × 5	4 × 432	781 × 5	3 × 623
4.	800 × 5	2 × 506	439 × 4	5 × 556
5.	249 × 3	5 × 361	968 × 4	2 × 704

6. There are 126 pins in one box.
   How many pins are there in 3 boxes?

7. A radio costs $262.
   A television set costs 4 times as much as the radio.
   How much does the television set cost?

8. Mrs Wang bought 3 boxes of beads.
   There were 260 beads in each box.
   How many beads did she buy altogether?

9. One packet of biscuits weighs 250 g.
   What is the total weight of 5 packets of biscuits?

10. Mrs Chen sold 680 eggs last week.
    She sold 4 times as many eggs this week as last week.
    How many eggs did she sell altogether?

11. The refrigerator costs 5 times as much as the rice cooker.
    What is the total cost of the refrigerator and the rice
    cooker?

PRACTICE 3F

Find the value of each of the following:

	(a)	(b)	(c)	(d)
1.	12 × 2	3 × 14	16 × 5	4 × 18
2.	223 × 2	4 × 527	129 × 2	3 × 326
3.	252 × 3	4 × 763	372 × 5	3 × 284
4.	724 × 2	3 × 105	414 × 4	5 × 120
5.	260 × 3	5 × 415	509 × 5	4 × 309

6. Mrs Fu made 280 egg sandwiches for a party.
   She made 3 times as many chicken sandwiches as egg sandwiches.
   How many chicken sandwiches did she make?

7. There are 365 days in a year.
   How many days are there in 4 years?

8. A pilot flies 105 hours in one month.
   How many hours will he fly in 5 months?

9. One box of chocolates weighs 350 g.
   Find the total weight of 2 boxes of chocolates.

10. There were 30 cakes in one box.
    Mrs Wu bought 4 boxes of cakes.
    How much did she pay for the cakes if each cake cost $3.

11. There are 18 chairs in the first row.
    There are 25 chairs in each of the other 5 rows.
    How many chairs are there altogether?

56

4 Quotient and Remainder

Meihua has 14 toy soldiers.
She puts the toy soldiers equally into 4 tents.
How many soldiers are there in each tent?
How many soldiers are left?

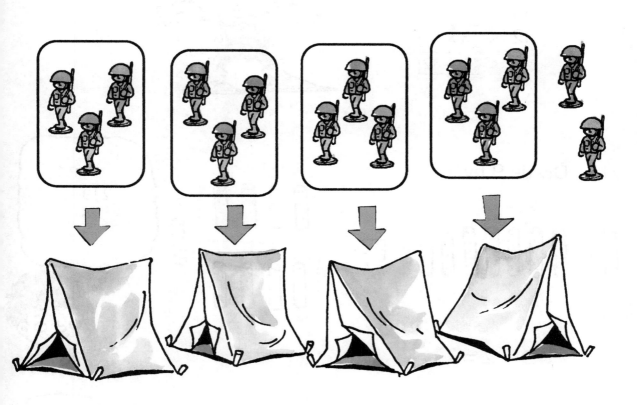

14 ÷ 4 = 3 with remainder 2

We write:
14 ÷ 4 = 3 R 2

There are ▊ soldiers in each tent.
▊ soldiers are left.

When 14 is divided by 4, the **quotient** is 3 and the **remainder** is 2.

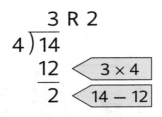

```
    3 R 2
4 ) 14
    12      ← 3 × 4
    ─
     2      ← 14 − 12
```

1. Divide 9 by 2.

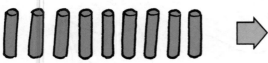

```
    4 R 1
2 ) 9
    8
    ─
    1
```

$$9 \div 2 = \blacksquare$$

2. Divide 12 by 2.

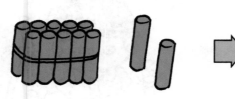
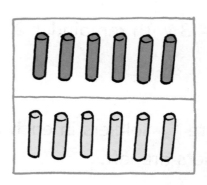

```
    6
2 ) 12
    12
    ──
     0
```

$$12 \div 2 = \blacksquare$$

3. 28 ÷ 2 =

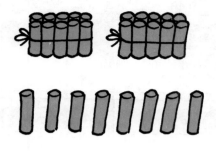

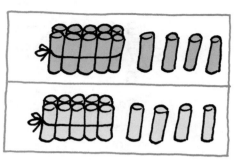

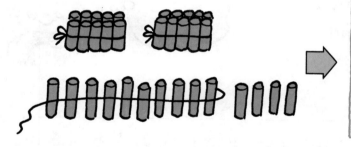

$$\begin{array}{r} 1 \\ 2{\overline{\smash{)}28}} \\ \underline{2} \\ \end{array}$$

$$\begin{array}{r} 14 \\ 2{\overline{\smash{)}28}} \\ \underline{2} \\ 8 \\ \underline{8} \\ 0 \end{array}$$

2 tens ÷ 2 = 1 ten   **8 ones ÷ 2 = 4 ones**

4. 34 ÷ 2 =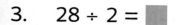

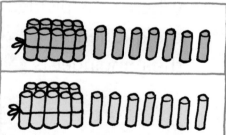

$$\begin{array}{r} 1 \\ 2{\overline{\smash{)}34}} \\ \underline{2} \\ 1 \end{array}$$

$$\begin{array}{r} 17 \\ 2{\overline{\smash{)}34}} \\ \underline{2} \\ 14 \\ \underline{14} \\ 0 \end{array}$$

3 tens ÷ 2 = 1 ten   **14 ones ÷ 2 = 7 ones**
with remainder 1 ten

5. $73 \div 2 = $

$$\begin{array}{r} 3 \\ 2\overline{)73} \\ 6 \\ \hline 1 \end{array}$$

⬇

$$\begin{array}{r} 36 \\ 2\overline{)73} \\ 6 \\ \hline 13 \\ 12 \\ \hline 1 \end{array}$$

Tens	Ones
10 10 10 10 10 10 10	1 1 1

Tens	Ones
10 10 10 10 10 10	1 1 1 1 1 1 1 1 1 1 1 1 1

$$\begin{array}{r} 36 \text{ R } 1 \\ 2\overline{)73} \\ 6 \\ \hline 13 \\ 12 \\ \hline 1 \end{array}$$

When 73 is divided by 2,
the quotient is ▇ and
the remainder is ▇.

6. Numbers in which the ones digit is **0, 2, 4, 6** or **8** are called **even numbers**.
Numbers in which the ones digit is **1, 3, 5, 7** or **9** are called **odd numbers**.

What can you say about the remainder in each of the following?
(a) an even number divided by 2
(b) an odd number divided by 2

Workbook Exercise 25

5 Dividing Hundreds, Tens and Ones

$400 \div 2 = \blacksquare$

4 hundreds ÷ 2

$500 \div 2 = \blacksquare$

5 hundreds ÷ 2

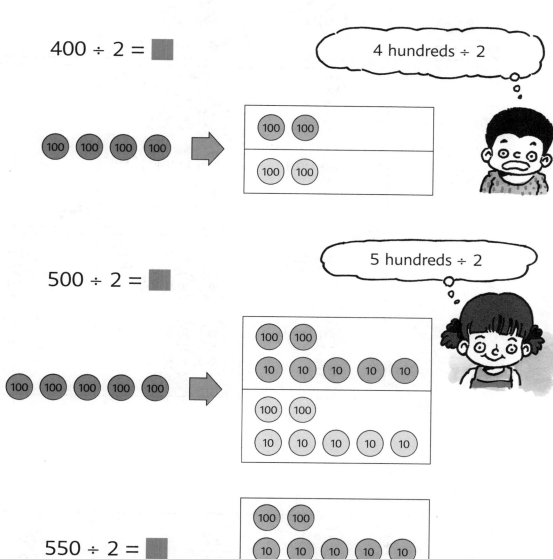

$550 \div 2 = \blacksquare$

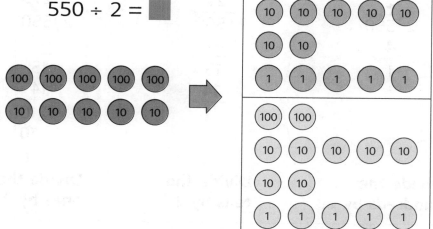

Hundreds	Tens	Ones

$2\overline{)550}$

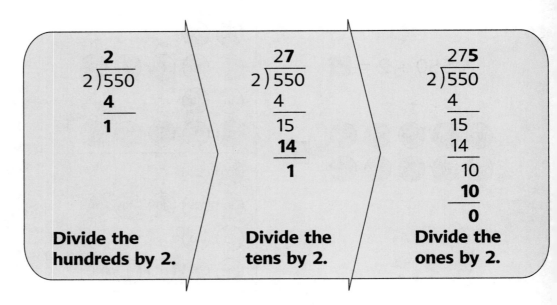

2	**27**	**275**
$2\overline{)550}$	$2\overline{)550}$	$2\overline{)550}$
4	4	4
1	15	15
	14	14
	1	10
		10
		0
Divide the hundreds by 2.	**Divide the tens by 2.**	**Divide the ones by 2.**

62

1. $96 \div 4 = $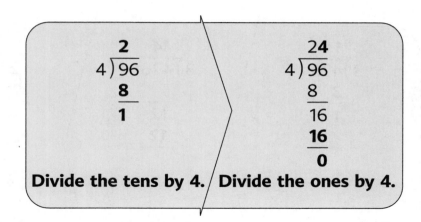

When 96 is divided by 4, the quotient is ▨ and the remainder is ▨.

2. $80 \div 3 = $ ▨

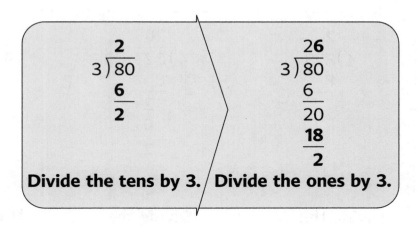

When 80 is divided by 3, the quotient is ▨ and the remainder is ▨.

3. Find the quotient and remainder for each of the following:
   (a) $48 \div 2$ (b) $60 \div 3$ (c) $54 \div 3$
   (d) $51 \div 4$ (e) $75 \div 5$ (f) $67 \div 5$

Workbook Exercise 26

4. $426 \div 3 = \blacksquare$

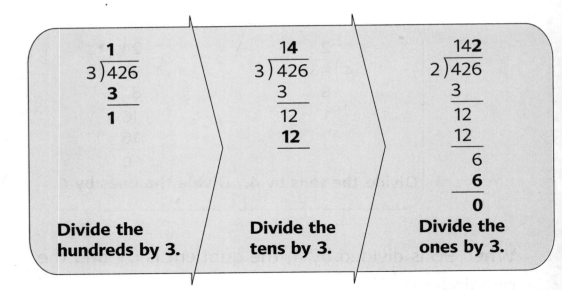

5. $823 \div 4 = \blacksquare$

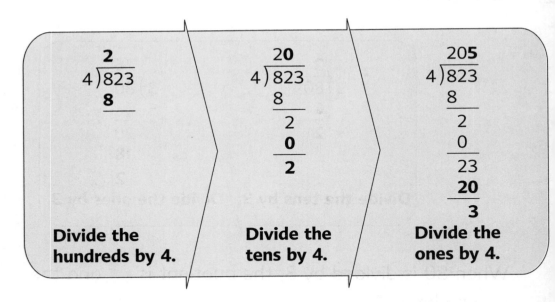

6. Find the quotient and remainder for each of the following:
    (a) $352 \div 4$ (b) $640 \div 2$ (c) $433 \div 5$
    (d) $700 \div 3$ (e) $290 \div 4$ (f) $105 \div 3$
    (g) $249 \div 4$ (h) $374 \div 2$ (i) $511 \div 5$

Workbook Exercise 27

PRACTICE 3G

Find the value of each of the following:

	(a)	(b)	(c)	(d)
1.	82 ÷ 2	58 ÷ 3	76 ÷ 1	80 ÷ 5
2.	91 ÷ 4	60 ÷ 4	37 ÷ 3	47 ÷ 3
3.	192 ÷ 2	702 ÷ 4	299 ÷ 5	429 ÷ 5
4.	600 ÷ 3	853 ÷ 2	330 ÷ 4	501 ÷ 3
5.	745 ÷ 5	900 ÷ 4	413 ÷ 3	123 ÷ 4

6. Aminah made 205 pancakes.
   She put them into boxes of 4 each.
   How many boxes of pancakes were there?
   How many pancakes were left over?

7. 5 packets of coffee powder weigh 750 g.
   How much does each packet weigh?

8. A man has 316 fishballs.
   He puts 3 fishballs on a stick.
   How many sticks of fishballs can he make?
   How many fishballs will be left over?

9. David has 74 wheels.
   If he uses 4 wheels to make a toy car, how
   many toy cars can he make?
   How many wheels will be left over?

10. Samad has 429 m of wire.
    He cuts it into pieces.
    Each piece is 3 m long.
    How many pieces can he get?

PRACTICE 3H

Find the value of each of the following:

	(a)	(b)	(c)	(d)
1.	20 × 5	42 ÷ 2	4 × 51	75 ÷ 3
2.	37 × 3	50 ÷ 5	2 × 78	60 ÷ 5
3.	312 × 4	123 ÷ 3	5 × 500	408 ÷ 4
4.	691 × 5	270 ÷ 4	3 × 607	500 ÷ 3
5.	768 × 3	679 ÷ 5	5 × 705	328 ÷ 5

6. A farmer keeps 64 goats.
   He keeps 5 times as many cows as goats.
   How many cows does he keep?

7. Mary works in a restaurant for 4 hours a day.
   (a) How many hours does she work in 26 days?
   (b) If she is paid $3 an hour, how much money does she earn in 26 days?

8. 5 boys share 150 Malaysian stamps and 200 Indonesian stamps equally.
   How many stamps of each country does each boy get?

9. Mr Tan packed 215 oranges into bags of 5 each.
   He sold all the oranges at $2 a bag.
   How much money did he receive?

10. David wants to buy 4 basketballs.
    He has only $55.
    How much more money does he need?

$18 each

REVIEW A

Find the value of each of the following:

	(a)	(b)	(c)
1.	1672 + 298	3984 + 1479	804 + 9196
2.	3941 − 296	4732 − 2415	5000 − 4999
3.	47 × 3	207 × 5	789 × 4
4.	78 ÷ 3	700 ÷ 4	451 ÷ 5

5. 1628 boys and 1092 girls took part in an art competition.
   How many children took part altogether?

6. There were 4525 concert tickets for sale in the morning.
   1909 tickets were sold at the end of the day.
   How many tickets were left?

7. There were 485 ℓ of petrol in one drum.
   How many litres of petrol were there in 4 drums?

8. (a) A tailor bought 563 m of cloth to make dresses.
       He used 3 m to make each dress.
       How many dresses did he make?
       How many metres of cloth were left?
   (b) If he sold all the dresses at $5 each, how much money
       did he receive?

9. There were 1052 people in a village.
   650 of them moved to a new town.
   226 of the people left in the village
   were adults.
   How many of them were children?

10. Sulin has $240.
    Meifen has 3 times as much money as Sulin.
    How much money do they have altogether?

Multiplication Tables of 6, 7, 8 and 9

1 **Looking Back**

1 × 1	1 × 2	1 × 3	1 × 4	1 × 5
2 × 1	2 × 2	2 × 3	2 × 4	2 × 5
3 × 1	3 × 2	3 × 3	3 × 4	3 × 5
4 × 1	4 × 2	4 × 3	4 × 4	4 × 5
5 × 1	5 × 2	5 × 3	5 × 4	5 × 5
6 × 1	6 × 2	6 × 3	6 × 4	6 × 5
7 × 1	7 × 2	7 × 3	7 × 4	7 × 5
8 × 1	8 × 2	8 × 3	8 × 4	8 × 5
9 × 1	9 × 2	9 × 3	9 × 4	9 × 5
10 × 1	10 × 2	10 × 3	10 × 4	10 × 5

Pick a card and give the answer.

Make the cards. Each of them has the answer at the back.

2×5
Front

10
Back

1×6	1×7	1×8	1×9	1×10
2×6	2×7	2×8	2×9	2×10
3×6	3×7	3×8	3×9	3×10
4×6	4×7	4×8	4×9	4×10
5×6	5×7	5×8	5×9	5×10
6×6	6×7	6×8	6×9	6×10
7×6	7×7	7×8	7×9	7×10
8×6	8×7	8×8	8×9	8×10
9×6	9×7	9×8	9×9	9×10
10×6	10×7	10×8	10×9	10×10

Do you know the answers of all the cards.

Workbook Exercise 28

2 Multiplying and Dividing by 6

The machine multiplies the number we put in by 6.

$3 \times 6 = \blacksquare$

The machine divides the number we put in by 6.

$30 \div 6 = \blacksquare$

1. (a)

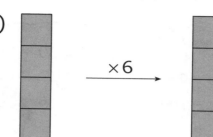

$4 \times 6 = $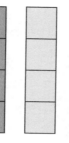

(b)

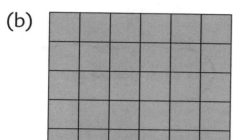

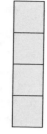

$5 \times 6 = 6 \times 5$

$5 \times 6 = $ ▢
$6 \times 5 = $ ▢

2. (a)

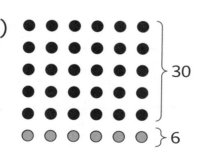

$6 \times 6 = 30 + 6$

$6 \times 5 = 30$
$6 \times 6 = $ ▢

(b)

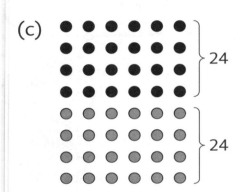

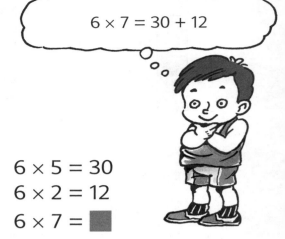

$6 \times 7 = 30 + 12$

$6 \times 5 = 30$
$6 \times 2 = 12$
$6 \times 7 = \blacksquare$

(c)

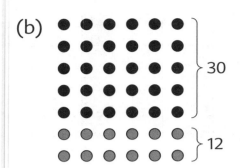

$6 \times 8 = 24 \times 2$

$6 \times 4 = 24$
$6 \times 8 = \blacksquare$

(d)

$6 \times 9 = 60 - 6$

$6 \times 10 = 60$
$6 \times 9 = \blacksquare$

3. Complete the number sentences.

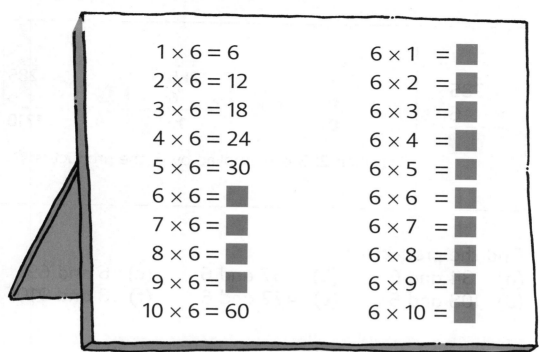

$1 \times 6 = 6$ $6 \times 1 \ = \blacksquare$

$2 \times 6 = 12$ $6 \times 2 \ = \blacksquare$

$3 \times 6 = 18$ $6 \times 3 \ = \blacksquare$

$4 \times 6 = 24$ $6 \times 4 \ = \blacksquare$

$5 \times 6 = 30$ $6 \times 5 \ = \blacksquare$

$6 \times 6 = \blacksquare$ $6 \times 6 \ = \blacksquare$

$7 \times 6 = \blacksquare$ $6 \times 7 \ = \blacksquare$

$8 \times 6 = \blacksquare$ $6 \times 8 \ = \blacksquare$

$9 \times 6 = \blacksquare$ $6 \times 9 \ = \blacksquare$

$10 \times 6 = 60$ $6 \times 10 = \blacksquare$

Workbook Exercise 29

4.

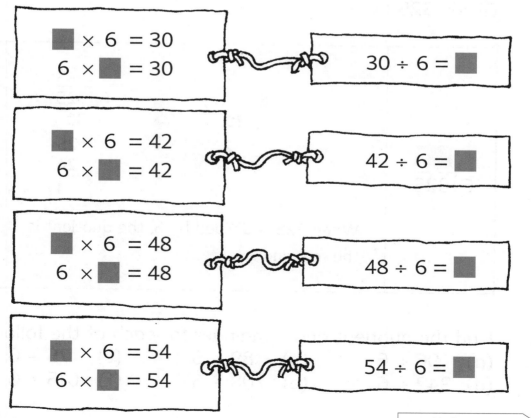

$\blacksquare \times 6 \ = 30$
$6 \ \times \blacksquare = 30$

$30 \div 6 = \blacksquare$

$\blacksquare \times 6 \ = 42$
$6 \ \times \blacksquare = 42$

$42 \div 6 = \blacksquare$

$\blacksquare \times 6 \ = 48$
$6 \ \times \blacksquare = 48$

$48 \div 6 = \blacksquare$

$\blacksquare \times 6 \ = 54$
$6 \ \times \blacksquare = 54$

$54 \div 6 = \blacksquare$

Workbook Exercise 30

5. Multiply 285 by 6.

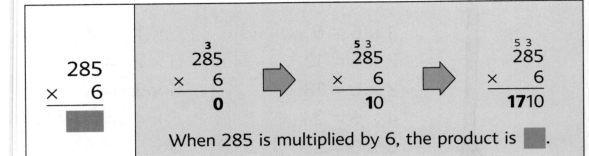

6. Find the product of
    (a)   34 and 6   (b)   57 and 6   (c) 6 and 69
    (d) 108 and 6   (e) 472 and 6   (f) 6 and 910

Workbook Exercise 31

7. Divide 325 by 6.

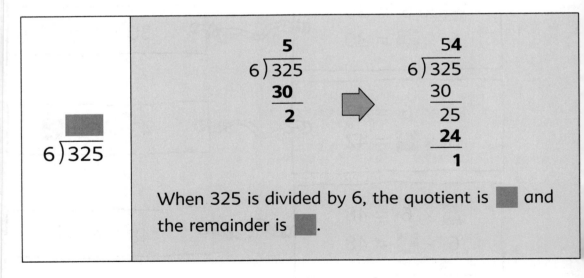

8. Find the quotient and remainder for each of the following:
    (a)   96 ÷ 6   (b)   89 ÷ 6   (c)   75 ÷ 6
    (d) 342 ÷ 6   (e) 708 ÷ 6   (f) 615 ÷ 6

Workbook Exercises 32 & 33

PRACTICE 4A

Find the value of each of the following:

	(a)	(b)	(c)
1.	6×3	6×4	7×6
2.	$18 \div 6$	$24 \div 6$	$42 \div 6$
3.	43×6	94×6	6×57
4.	$80 \div 6$	$405 \div 6$	$562 \div 6$

5. Find the missing numbers.

   (a) $6 \times \blacksquare = 36$ (b) $\blacksquare \times 4 = 24$

   (c) $7 \times \blacksquare = 42$ (d) $\blacksquare \times 6 = 60$

6. There are 6 players in one team.
   How many players are there in 14 teams?

7. 6 children share 84 balloons equally.
   How many balloons does each child get?

8. John earns $85 a week.
   How much money can he earn in 6 weeks?

9. Mr Lin tied 192 books into bundles of 6 each.
   How many bundles were there?

10. Cik Halimah bought 6 m of cloth for $84.
    Find the cost of 5 m of cloth.

11. Encik Ahmad bought 6 kg of durians.
    1 kg of durians cost $6.
    How much did he pay?

3 Multiplying and Dividing by 7

Mr Samy made this table to help him collect money.

Number of cakes	1	2	3	4	5
Cost	$7	$14	$21	$28	$35

(a) Aihua bought 2 cakes.
    How much did she pay?
(b) Mrs Li ordered 4 cakes for a party.
    How much did she pay?
(c) Siti paid Mr Samy $35.
    How many cakes did Mr Samy give her?
(d) How many cakes could Mr Fu buy with $42?

1. (a)

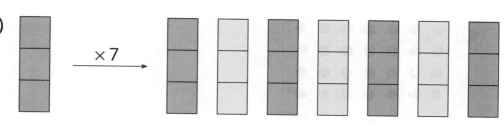

$3 \times 7 = \blacksquare$

(b)

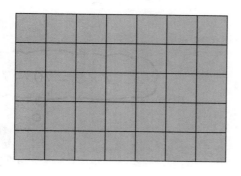

$5 \times 7 = \blacksquare$

$7 \times 5 = \blacksquare$

2. (a)

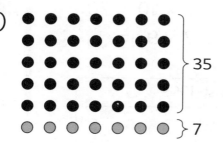

}35

}7

$7 \times 6 = 35 + 7$

$7 \times 5 = 35$

$7 \times 6 = \blacksquare$

(b)

}35

}14

$7 \times 7 = 35 + 14$

$7 \times 5 = 35$

$7 \times 2 = 14$

$7 \times 7 = \blacksquare$

(c)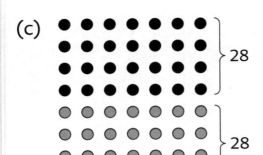

$7 \times 4 = 28$

$7 \times 8 = \blacksquare$

(d)

70

$7 \times 9 = 70 - 7$

$7 \times 10 = 70$

$7 \times 9 \ = \blacksquare$

3.

August 1999						
S	M	T	W	T	F	S
1	2	3	4	5	6	7
8	9	10	11	12	13	14
15	16	17	18	19	20	21
22	23	24	25	26	27	28
29	30	31				

There are 7 days in a week.

There are ■ days in 2 weeks.

There are ■ days in 4 weeks.

There are ■ days in 10 weeks.

4. Complete the number sentences.

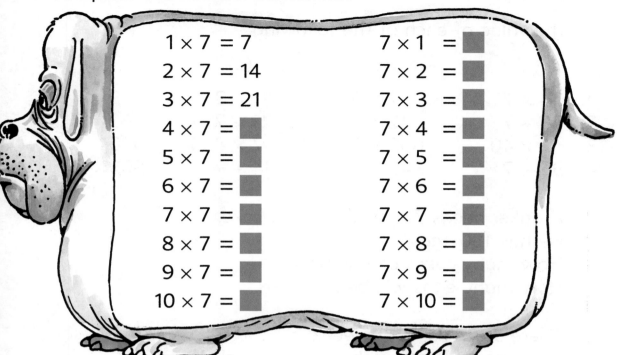

$1 \times 7 = 7$ $7 \times 1 = \blacksquare$

$2 \times 7 = 14$ $7 \times 2 = \blacksquare$

$3 \times 7 = 21$ $7 \times 3 = \blacksquare$

$4 \times 7 = \blacksquare$ $7 \times 4 = \blacksquare$

$5 \times 7 = \blacksquare$ $7 \times 5 = \blacksquare$

$6 \times 7 = \blacksquare$ $7 \times 6 = \blacksquare$

$7 \times 7 = \blacksquare$ $7 \times 7 = \blacksquare$

$8 \times 7 = \blacksquare$ $7 \times 8 = \blacksquare$

$9 \times 7 = \blacksquare$ $7 \times 9 = \blacksquare$

$10 \times 7 = \blacksquare$ $7 \times 10 = \blacksquare$

5. Find the value of
   (a) 6×7 (b) 7×7 (c) 7×9
   (d) $56 \div 7$ (e) $70 \div 7$ (f) $21 \div 7$

Workbook Exercise 34

6. Multiply.
   (a) 56×7 (b) 63×7 (c) 7×71
   (d) 920×7 (e) 804×7 (f) 7×218

Workbook Exercise 35

7. Divide.
   (a) $75 \div 7$ (b) $84 \div 7$ (c) $64 \div 7$
   (d) $91 \div 7$ (e) $98 \div 7$ (f) $80 \div 7$

8. Divide.
   (a) $108 \div 7$ (b) $231 \div 7$ (c) $682 \div 7$
   (d) $730 \div 7$ (e) $954 \div 7$ (f) $705 \div 7$

Workbook Exercises 36 & 37

PRACTICE 4B

Find the value of each of the following:

	(a)	(b)	(c)	(d)
1.	4×7	7×6	7×3	9×7
2.	$28 \div 7$	$42 \div 7$	$21 \div 7$	$63 \div 7$
3.	7×40	608×7	7×800	930×7
4.	$95 \div 7$	$540 \div 7$	$714 \div 7$	$805 \div 7$

5. A baker needs 7 eggs to bake a cake.
    He has 150 eggs.
    How many cakes can he bake?
    How many eggs will be left over?

6. There are 7 days in a week.
    How many days are there in 52 weeks?

7. Mr Wong is 7 times as old as his grandson
    He is 63 years old.
    How old is his grandson?

8. 1 kg of prawns cost $26.
    Mr Chen bought 7 kg of prawns.
    How much did he pay?

1kg - $26

9. Cik Siti spent $84 on 7 towels.
    What was the cost of 1 towel?

10. Mrs Li packed 112 lemons into bags of 7 each.
    She sold all the lemons at $3 a bag.
    How much money did she receive?

11. A jacket cost 7 times as much as a T-shirt.
    If the T-shirt cost $26, what was the total cost of the T-shirt
    and the jacket?

PRACTICE 4C

Find the value of each of the following:

	(a)	(b)	(c)	(d)
1.	6 × 6	7 × 8	6 × 10	7 × 7
2.	36 ÷ 6	42 ÷ 6	60 ÷ 6	49 ÷ 7
3.	67 × 7	0 × 7	10 × 1	513 × 7
4.	304 ÷ 6	0 ÷ 7	10 ÷ 10	847 ÷ 7

5. Meili has a piece of rope 161 cm long.
   She cuts it into 7 equal pieces.
   What is the length of each piece?

6. Mr Wang bought 28 kg of durians.
   How much did he spend?

7. A baker bought 84 eggs to bake cakes.
   He used 6 eggs to bake each cake.
   How many cakes did he bake?

8. 6 children shared 3 boxes of cookies equally.
   Each box contained 48 cookies.
   How many cookies did each child get?

9. There were 7 boxes of blue pens and red pens.
   There were 12 pens in each box.
   If there were 36 red pens, how many blue pens were there?

10. Mrs Wu bought 35 m of cloth at $6 for 1 m.
    She still had $25 left after paying for the cloth.
    How much did she have at first?

4 Multiplying and Dividing by 8

$\times 2$ $\times 2$

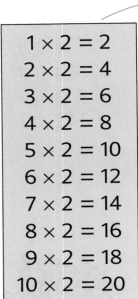

$1 \times 2 = 2$	$1 \times 4 = 4$	$1 \times 8 = 8$
$2 \times 2 = 4$	$2 \times 4 = 8$	$2 \times 8 = 16$
$3 \times 2 = 6$	$3 \times 4 = 12$	$3 \times 8 = 24$
$4 \times 2 = 8$	$4 \times 4 = 16$	$4 \times 8 = 32$
$5 \times 2 = 10$	$5 \times 4 = 20$	$5 \times 8 = 40$
$6 \times 2 = 12$	$6 \times 4 = 24$	$6 \times 8 = 48$
$7 \times 2 = 14$	$7 \times 4 = 28$	$7 \times 8 = 56$
$8 \times 2 = 16$	$8 \times 4 = 32$	$8 \times 8 = \blacksquare$
$9 \times 2 = 18$	$9 \times 4 = 36$	$9 \times 8 = \blacksquare$
$10 \times 2 = 20$	$10 \times 4 = 40$	$10 \times 8 = 80$

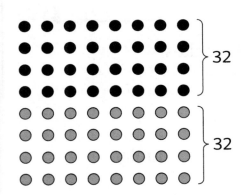

$8 \times 4 = 32$

$8 \times 8 = \blacksquare$

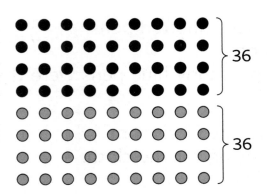

$9 \times 4 = 36$

$9 \times 8 = \blacksquare$

1. An octopus has 8 arms.

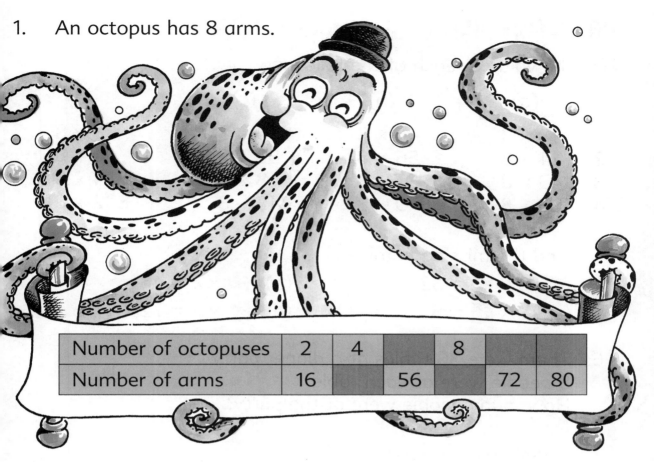

Number of octopuses	2	4		8		
Number of arms	16		56		72	80

2. Multiply.
   (a) 3×8 (b) 5×8 (c) 8×8
   (d) 8×4 (e) 8×7 (f) 8×9

3. Divide.
   (a) $80 \div 8$ (b) $48 \div 8$ (c) $24 \div 8$
   (d) $72 \div 8$ (e) $56 \div 8$ (f) $40 \div 8$

   Workbook Exercise 38

4. Multiply.
   (a) 56×8 (b) 79×8 (c) 8×68
   (d) 418×8 (e) 305×8 (f) 8×620

   Workbook Exercise 39

5. Divide.
   (a) $98 \div 8$ (b) $112 \div 8$ (c) $807 \div 8$
   (d) $305 \div 8$ (e) $664 \div 8$ (f) $960 \div 8$

   Workbook Exercises 40 & 41

PRACTICE 4D

Find the value of each of the following:

	(a)	(b)	(c)	(d)
1.	8×3	6×8	10×8	8×8
2.	$24 \div 8$	$56 \div 8$	$80 \div 8$	$64 \div 8$
3.	43×8	97×8	8×262	874×8
4.	$120 \div 8$	$579 \div 8$	$745 \div 8$	$832 \div 8$

5. Find the missing numbers.

   (a) $8 \times \blacksquare = 32$ (b) $\blacksquare \times 8 = 48$

   (c) $8 \times \blacksquare = 64$ (d) $\blacksquare \times 8 = 72$

6. There were 36 tables at a dinner party.
   8 people were at each table.
   How many people were at the party?

7. A pail holds 18 litres.
   8 pails of water can fill a tank.
   How many litres of water does the tank hold

8. Mrs Fu baked 390 tarts.
   She put them into packets of 8 each.
   How many packets did she have?
   How many tarts were left over?

9. A gardener bought 12 watering cans.
   Each can cost $8.
   If he gave the cashier $100, how much change did he
   receive?

10. Mrs Wong bought a refrigerator.
    She paid $245 in the first month and $103 each month for
    another 8 months.
    What was the cost of the refrigerator?

PRACTICE 4E

Find the value of each of the following:

	(a)	(b)	(c)	(d)
1.	6 × 7	7 × 8	8 × 10	8 × 9
2.	42 ÷ 6	56 ÷ 7	48 ÷ 8	72 ÷ 8
3.	73 ÷ 7	1 × 8	0 × 8	150 ÷ 8
4.	943 ÷ 8	8 ÷ 1	0 ÷ 8	872 ÷ 6

5. A grocer had 145 kg of sugar.
   He packed the sugar into packets of 6 kg each.
   How many packets were there?
   How many kilograms of sugar were left over?

6. Mr Chen wants to buy
   umbrellas.
   Each umbrella costs $7.
   How many umbrellas can he
   buy with $168?

7. There are 120 pages in an exercise book.
   How many pages are there in 8 exercise books?

8. Mr Tan wants to buy 6 chairs which cost $28 each.
   He has only $100.
   How much more money does he need?

9. 8 people went to the seaside.
   They hired a boat for 6 hours.
   If they shared the cost equally, how
   much did each person spend?

⑤ Multiplying and Dividing by 9

$1 \times 10 = 10$	$1 \times 9 = 9$
$2 \times 10 = 20$	$2 \times 9 = 18$
$3 \times 10 = 30$	$3 \times 9 = 27$
$4 \times 10 = 40$	$4 \times 9 = 36$
$5 \times 10 = 50$	$5 \times 9 = 45$
$6 \times 10 = 60$	$6 \times 9 = 54$
$7 \times 10 = 70$	$7 \times 9 = 63$
$8 \times 10 = 80$	$8 \times 9 = \blacksquare$
$9 \times 10 = 90$	$9 \times 9 = \blacksquare$
$10 \times 10 = 100$	$10 \times 9 = 90$

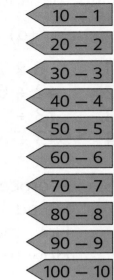

$10 - 1$
$20 - 2$
$30 - 3$
$40 - 4$
$50 - 5$
$60 - 6$
$70 - 7$
$80 - 8$
$90 - 9$
$100 - 10$

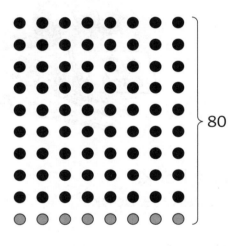

80

$8 \times 10 = 80$
$8 \times 9 \ = \blacksquare$

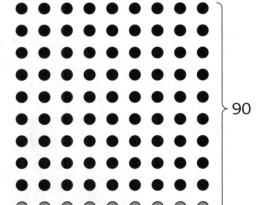

90

$9 \times 10 = 90$
$9 \times 9 \ = \blacksquare$

1. Add the tens digit and ones digit of each product.
   The answer is ▮.

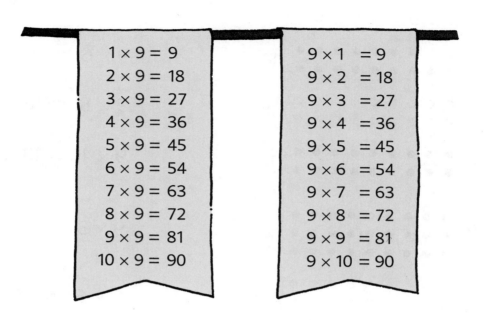

$1 \times 9 = 9$	$9 \times 1 = 9$
$2 \times 9 = 18$	$9 \times 2 = 18$
$3 \times 9 = 27$	$9 \times 3 = 27$
$4 \times 9 = 36$	$9 \times 4 = 36$
$5 \times 9 = 45$	$9 \times 5 = 45$
$6 \times 9 = 54$	$9 \times 6 = 54$
$7 \times 9 = 63$	$9 \times 7 = 63$
$8 \times 9 = 72$	$9 \times 8 = 72$
$9 \times 9 = 81$	$9 \times 9 = 81$
$10 \times 9 = 90$	$9 \times 10 = 90$

2. Here is an interesting way to multiply by 9.

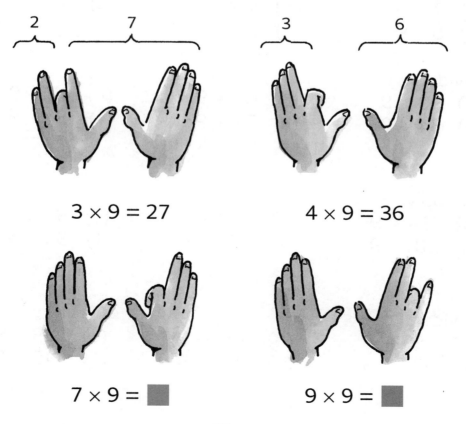

$3 \times 9 = 27$ $4 \times 9 = 36$

$7 \times 9 =$ ▮ $9 \times 9 =$ ▮

3. (a)

$9 \times 2 = 18$

$9 \times 4 = 18 \times \blacksquare$

$9 \times 6 = 18 \times \blacksquare$

$9 \times 8 = 18 \times \blacksquare$

$9 \times 10 = 18 \times \blacksquare$

(b)

$9 \times 3 = 27$

$9 \times 6 = 27 \times \blacksquare$

4. Multiply.
   (a) 2×9 (b) 4×9 (c) 9×3
   (d) 8×9 (e) 9×9 (f) 9×7

5. Divide.
   (a) $90 \div 9$ (b) $63 \div 9$ (c) $45 \div 9$
   (d) $54 \div 9$ (e) $72 \div 9$ (f) $81 \div 9$

   Workbook Exercise 42

6. Multiply.
   (a) 54×9 (b) 73×9 (c) 9×80
   (d) 201×9 (e) 678×9 (f) 9×609

   Workbook Exercise 43

7. Divide.
   (a) $97 \div 9$ (b) $108 \div 9$ (c) $89 \div 9$
   (d) $620 \div 9$ (e) $903 \div 9$ (f) $145 \div 9$

   Workbook Exercises 44 & 45

PRACTICE 4F

Find the value of each of the following:

	(a)	(b)	(c)	(d)
1.	3 × 9	9 × 4	9 × 5	9 × 9
2.	27 ÷ 9	36 ÷ 9	45 ÷ 9	81 ÷ 9
3.	36 × 9	9 × 400	657 × 9	198 × 9
4.	954 ÷ 9	563 ÷ 9	790 ÷ 9	823 ÷ 9

5. Mary bought 9 pieces of string each 18 m long.
   How many metres of string did she buy?

6. 25 boys went camping.
   Each boy brought 9 cans of food.
   How many cans did they bring altogether?

7. Gopal bought 9 T-shirts for $144.
   How much did one T-shirt cost?

8. David cut a wire 918 m long into pieces.
   Each piece was 9 m long.
   How many pieces did he get?

9. Hassan uses 185 ℓ of petrol a month.
   How much petrol does he use in 9 months?

10. A tailor bought 9 packets of buttons.
    There were 120 buttons in each packet.
    He used 8 buttons on a dress.
    How many dresses did he make if he used all the buttons?

11. Meihua bought 27 apples at 3 for $2.
    How much did she pay in all?

PRACTICE 4G

Find the value of each of the following:

	(a)	(b)	(c)	(d)
1.	9×6	7×10	8×8	6×6
2.	$54 \div 6$	$70 \div 7$	$64 \div 8$	$36 \div 6$
3.	69×8	1×9	0×9	901×6
4.	$581 \div 9$	$9 \div 1$	$0 \div 9$	$749 \div 7$

5. Mrs Wang gives each of her children $7.
   If she gives a total of $28 to her children, how many children does she have?

6. A tank holds 126 litres.
   A pail holds 9 litres.
   How many pails of water will fill up the tank?

7. Mingfa worked for 7 days.
   He was paid $36 each day.
   How much money did he receive?

8. There are 136 roses.
   There are 6 times as many sunflowers as roses.
   How many sunflowers are there?

9. Mr Lin had 112 tomatoes.
   8 of them were rotten.
   He packed the good tomatoes into packets of 8 each.
   How many packets of tomatoes did he get?

10. There were 8 stamps in a set.
    Gopal bought 120 sets of stamps.
    After selling some stamps, he had 680 stamps left.
    How many stamps did he sell?

5

Money

1 Dollars and Cents

Read the prices of these items.

$35.25

$35   25¢

The dot . separates the cents from the dollars.

$35.25

$35.25 = ▮ dollars ▮ cents

$67.25

$67.25 = ▮ dollars ▮ cents

$75.40

$75.40 = ▮ dollars ▮ cents

$32.75

$32.75 = ▮ dollars ▮ cents

91

1. How much money is there in each set?

   (a)

   ▓ dollars ▓ cents = $ ▓

   (b)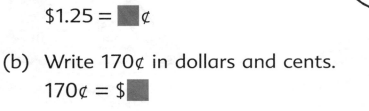

   ▓ dollars ▓ cents = $ ▓

2. (a) Write $1.25 in cents.

   $1.25 = ▓ ¢

   (b) Write 170¢ in dollars and cents.

   170¢ = $ ▓

   $1 = 100¢

3. Write in cents.
   (a) $0.30   (b) $1.95   (c) $4.05

4. Write in dollars and cents.
   (a) 85¢   (b) 160¢   (c) 345¢

5. How much more money is needed to make $1?
   (a) $0.70 + $ ▓ = $1   (b) $0.55 + $ ▓ = $1

Workbook Exercise 46

PRACTICE 5A

1. Write in cents.
   (a) $0.20   (b) $0.65   (c) $7.00
   (d) $2.05   (e) $5.60   (f) $3.95

2. Write in dollars and cents.
   (a) 5¢   (b) 60¢   (c) 400¢
   (d) 210¢   (e) 855¢   (f) 305¢

3. Find the missing amount of money in each of the following:
   (a) 30¢ + ■ = $1   (b) ■ + 45¢ = $1
   (c) $0.40 + ■ = $1   (d) ■ + $0.65 = $1

4. (a)

   6 twenty-cent coins = $■

   (b)

   12 five-cent coins = $■

   (c) Lily has 6 twenty-cent coins and 12 five-cent coins.
       How much money does she have altogether?

5. There are 2 five-cent coins, 3 twenty-cent coins and
   4 one-dollar coins in a purse.
   What is the total amount of money in the purse?

② Addition

Mrs Chen bought a box of chocolates for $13.25 and a cake for $6.50.
How much did she spend altogether?

Cost of chocolates   Cost of cake

Total cost of chocolates and cake

$13.25 + $6.50 = $▇

She spent $▇ altogether.

94

1. Find the value of
   (a) $1.50 + 20¢
   (b) $14.20 + 65¢
   (c) $38.40 + 35¢
   (d) $2.75 + 25¢
   (e) $25.40 + 60¢
   (f) $33.85 + 15¢

2. (a) $2.85 + 20¢ = $▮
   (b) $2.70 + 60¢ = $▮
   (c) $5.65 + 45¢ = $▮
   (d) $16.95 + 45¢ = $▮
   (e) $24.70 + 95¢ = $▮

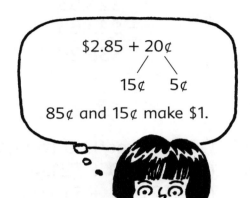

$2.85 + 20¢
/ \
15¢   5¢

85¢ and 15¢ make $1.

3. (a) $25.70 $\xrightarrow{+\ \$4}$ $▮ $\xrightarrow{+\ 10¢}$ $▮

   $25.70 + $4.10 = $▮

   (b) $34.65 $\xrightarrow{+\ \$2}$ $▮ $\xrightarrow{+\ 35¢}$ $▮

   $34.65 + $2.35 = $▮

   (c) $30.80 $\xrightarrow{+\ \$5}$ $▮ $\xrightarrow{+\ 40¢}$ $▮

   $30.80 + $5.40 = $▮

   (d) $24.70 $\xrightarrow{+\ \$10}$ $▮ $\xrightarrow{+\ 50¢}$ $▮

   $24.70 + $10.50 = $▮

4. Find the value of
   (a) $14.65 + $6.20
   (b) $13.60 + $24.40
   (c) $32.70 + $24.50
   (d) $15.60 + $23.70
   (e) $40.85 + $19.65
   (f) $28.35 + $26.75

5. We can add $24.55 and $13.65 like this:

$24.55
+ $ 13.65

$38.20

Use this method to find the value of
(a) $35.30 + $21.40
(b) $27.10 + $10.90
(c) $40.70 + $33.60
(d) $52.85 + $16.35
(e) $28.65 + $32.45
(f) $36.90 + $24.85

Workbook Exercise 47

6. Ali bought a toy car for $6.95.
He also spent $2.80 on a meal.
How much money did he spend altogether?

$2.80 + $6.95 = $

He spent $▮ altogether.

7. Mingfa paid $11.90 for a pen.
    He had $24.65 left.
    How much money did he have at first?

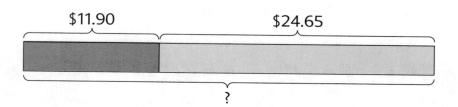

$11.90 + $24.65 = $⬛

He had $⬛ at first.

8. John saves $6.75 this week.
    He saves $2.35 less this week than last week.
    How much money did he save last week?

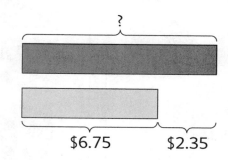

$6.75 + $2.35 = $⬛

He saved $⬛ last week.

Workbook Exercise 48

3 Subtraction

Mr Wu bought a radio and a calculator for $56.50.
The calculator cost $25.30.
How much did the radio cost?

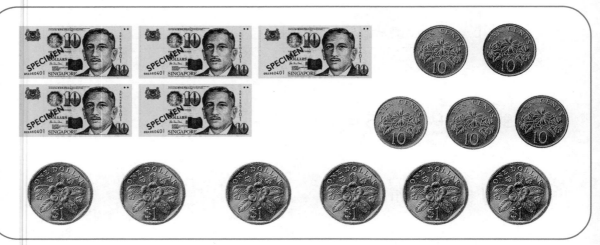

Cost of radio and calculator

Cost of calculator

Cost of radio

$56.50 − $25.30 = $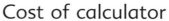

The radio cost $.

1. Find the value of
   (a) $2.60 − 20¢
   (c) $35.85 − 45¢
   (e) $6.50 − 45¢
   (b) $8.75 − 30¢
   (d) $1.50 − 25¢
   (f) $46.70 − 25¢

2. (a) $1 − 60¢ = ☐¢
   (c) $1.25 − 35¢ = ☐¢
   (b) $1.30 − 60¢ = ☐¢
   (d) $1.40 − 85¢ = ☐¢

3. (a) $3.20 − 80¢ = $☐
   (b) $14.65 − 90¢ = $☐
   (c) $46.25 − 45¢ = $☐
   (d) $32.05 − 85¢ = $☐
   (e) $42.30 − 55¢ = $☐

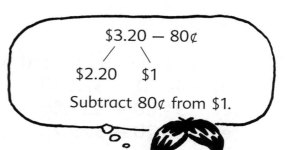

$3.20 − 80¢

$2.20 $1

Subtract 80¢ from $1.

4. (a) $16.80 —$4→ $☐ —60¢→ $☐

   $16.80 − $4.60 = $☐

   (b) $37.70 —$12→ $☐ —20¢→ $☐

   $37.70 − $10.20 = $☐

   (c) $29.20 —$12→ $☐ —50¢→ $☐

   $29.20 − $12.50 = $☐

5. Find the value of
   (a) $47.50 − $12
   (c) $58 − $12.60
   (e) $25.05 − $15.35
   (b) $35.70 − $0.85
   (d) $64.40 − $11.60
   (f) $56.20 − $28.95

6. We can subtract $23.70 from $46.20 like this:

$46.20
− $23.70

$22.50

$$\begin{array}{r} 4\,\overset{5\ 12}{\cancel{6}\,\cancel{2}}\,0 \\ -\ 2370 \\ \hline 2250 \end{array}$$

Use this method to find the value of
(a) $45.10 − $23.40   (b) $36.35 − $10.85
(c) $94.60 − $37.80   (d) $52.25 − $35.45
(e) $70.20 − $28.75   (f) $65.05 − $35.15

7. Find the value of
(a) 6200 − 415   (b) $62.00 − $4.15
(c) 4005 − 835   (d) $40.05 − $8.35

8. Find the value of
(a) $10 − $4.70   (b) $30 − $7.20   (c) $50 − $8.25
(d) $50 − $23.80 (e) $100 − $52.90 (f) $100 − $39.45

Workbook Exercise 49

9. Nancy bought a box of biscuits which cost $5.65.
She gave the cashier $10.
How much change did she receive?

$10 − $5.65 = $▆

She received $▆ change.

10. Meili had $20.
    She bought an umbrella and had $14.60 left.
    What was the cost of the umbrella?

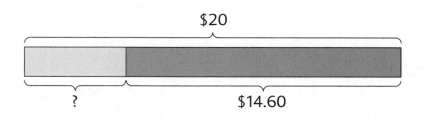

$20 − $14.60 = $ ▮

The umbrella cost $ ▮.

11. Minghua has $25.50.
    He wants to buy a watch which costs $35.
    How much more money does he need?

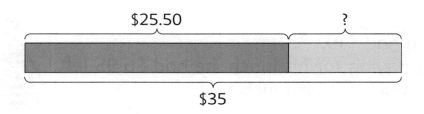

$35 − $25.50 = $ ▮

He needs $ ▮ more.

Workbook Exercises 50 & 51

PRACTICE 5B

1. Add.
   (a) $26.20 + $13.50
   (b) $39.45 + $60.55
   (c) $48.40 + $27.30
   (d) $15.95 + $24.35
   (e) $65.85 + $25.80
   (f) $36.45 + $54.55

2. Subtract.
   (a) $36.70 − $15.35
   (b) $60.50 − $24.45
   (c) $52.30 − $30.70
   (d) $40.05 − $16.30
   (e) $72.20 − $26.95
   (f) $81.00 − $31.85

3. After spending $24.60, Meihua had $76.40 left.
   How much money did she have at first?

4. Mingfa wants to buy a fishing rod which costs $62.50.
   He has only $48.60.
   How much more money does he need?

5. A toy car costs $16.80.
   A toy aeroplane costs $5.60 more than the toy car.
   What is the cost of the toy aeroplane?

6. Sumin had $10.
   After paying for his lunch, he had $6.95 left.
   How much did his lunch cost?

7. A blouse and a skirt cost $42.50.
   The blouse costs $16.85.
   What is the cost of the skirt?

8. Meilin had $40.50.
   She bought a pen for $6.80 and a book for $13.20.
   How much money had she left?

PRACTICE 5C

Find the value of each of the following:

	(a)	(b)
1.	$14.85 + $26.15	$25.60 − $22.35
2.	$29.65 + $0.95	$41.90 − $16.75
3.	$40.80 + $59.20	$50.00 − $31.05
4.	$34.45 + $28.95	$32.05 − $22.95
5.	$72.95 + $26.95	$64.25 − $35.95

6. A badminton racket costs $15.90.
   A tennis racket costs $42.50.
   How much cheaper is the badminton racket than the tennis racket?

7. The usual price of a radio is $43.
   Its sale price is $29.95.
   How much cheaper is the sale price than the usual price?

8. Sumei has $10.80.
   Her mother gives her some more money.
   She has $12.30 now.
   How much money has her mother given her?

9. Mr Chen bought some vegetables for $2.40 and a fish for $3.70.
   He had $21.30 left.
   How much money did he have at first?

10. Mrs Wu bought a chicken and a duck.
    The chicken cost $5.70.
    The duck cost $1.95 more than the chicken.
    How much did she spend altogether?

REVIEW B

Find the value of each of the following:

	(a)	(b)	(c)
1.	609 + 92	982 + 128	4976 + 24
2.	820 − 118	903 − 294	3005 − 2096
3.	49 × 6	204 × 7	382 × 9
4.	96 ÷ 6	104 ÷ 7	260 ÷ 8

5. Aihui worked in a factory for 9 days.
   She was paid $45 each day.
   How much did she earn altogether?

6. Mrs Raja paid $56 for some durians.
   How many kilograms of durians did
   she buy?

7. Lily weighs 29 kg.
   Her father is 3 times as heavy as she.
   How much heavier is Lily's father
   than Lily?

8. Mr Lin bought 2500 tiles.
   He used 1164 tiles for one room and 940 tiles for another
   room.
   How many tiles were left?

9. 4 people bought a birthday present for their friend.
   They paid the cashier $100 and received $48 change.
   If they shared the cost equally, how much did each person
   pay?

10. Cik Faridah bought 8 packets of biscuits for a party.
    There were 12 biscuits in each packet.
    After the party, there were 28 biscuits left.
    How many biscuits were eaten at the party?